SARADA DEVI

Holiness, Charisma and Iconic Motherhood

AMIYA P. SEN

PAPER MISSILE
NIYOGI BOOKS

Published by
NIYOGI BOOKS
Block D, Building No. 77,
Okhla Industrial Area, Phase-I,
New Delhi-110 020, INDIA
Tel: 91-11-26816301, 26818960
Email: niyogibooks@gmail.com
Website: www.niyogibooksindia.com

Editor: Arunima Ghosh
Layout: Shashi Bhushan Prasad
Cover design: Anurag Hira
Cover illustrator: Douluri Narayana

ISBN: 978-93-91125-70-7
Publication: 2022

Publisher's note: Every effort has been made to ensure the accuracy of the information presented in this book. The images used in this book come from either the public domain or from the public commons, unless otherwise stated. The publisher welcomes comments and feedback from readers, in order to improve future editions, at niyogibooks@gmail.com.

Printed at Niyogi Offset Pvt. Ltd., New Delhi, India

For

Dadu (Kamakhyaprosad Sen) &
Bodopishi (Binapani Sengupta)
whose love and affection for me was boundless

CONTENTS

PREFACE

For a modern professional, it would be irrational to suggest that some unknown or inscrutable force has guided his choices in writing historical biographies. Nonetheless, this is an eerie feeling that has increasingly seized me over the years and I am now learning to be at peace with it. I can also see that this works in mysterious ways. It arrives in the form of unexpected discussions with friends and colleagues who, whether fortuitously or not, air similar concerns or feelings on a subject. It also arrives in the form of completely unexpected encounters with rare books and other relevant source material. I could not believe my luck when several years back, while strolling along the Bowbazar Street in Kolkata, I found with a pavement book seller the first edition of Brahmachari Akshaychaitanya's biography of Sarada Devi, the first full length biography to be written on the Holy Mother. Even more unlikely was my discovery of a copy of Swami Hiranmayananda's *Sri Sarada: The Great Wonder* on a campus sale of books in Heidelberg. Rummaging through the family library one day, I discovered also an early edition of Swami Arupananda's two volume classic, *Sri Sri Mayer Kotha,* acquired possibly by my father. Earlier in my life, I had also similarly discovered the five volume set of the *Sri Sri Ramakrishna Kathamrita* published by the Kathamrita Bhavan. I felt blessed each time an incident of this kind occurred; the eerie feeling too would creep in silently.

Having worked at length on the life and logia of Sri Ramakrishna, it would have been only natural for me to turn my attention to Sarada Devi. However, things did not quite develop the way I anticipated. For one, the parables and preaching of Sri Ramakrishna as reported in the *Kathamrita* cast a great influence on me and there was really nothing within the available Sarada literature that could be taken to be as rich, influential or enduring. Second, until recently, biographical work on Sarada Devi was almost exclusively confined to the work of monk scholars where, predictably, the intent and tone was at times brazenly adulatory and hagiographic. Unlike what happened in the case of Ramakrishna, no independent scholar or even a lay devotee attempted to write a biographical work on Sarada or list her teachings. Third, Sarada Devi was never as celebrated in the Bengali language press as was Sri Ramakrishna in his time and thereafter. I know from personal experience that this dearth of alternative source material has discouraged some scholars and works of a more critical nature. Prof. Rajagopal Chattopadhyaya, the author of some refreshingly original and revisionist studies of Sri Ramakrishna, Swami Vivekananda and Sister Nivedita once admitted to me that he felt quite inhibited by the fact that there was no way of effectively corroborating claims made by monk biographers.

Such limitations that potential authors and biographers have struggled with only adds greater value to the work of the historian Narasingha P. Sil. In 2003, Sil produced the first critical biography of Sarada Devi, reportedly amidst some resistance and hostility from the Ramakrishna Mission. Apparently, Prof. Sil did not feel deterred by constraints of source material. I have reason to thank him both for demonstrating ways of overcoming such constraints and for providing a valuable sounding board to test my own arguments and theories. On the subject of Sarada Devi, I have profited as much from reading Prof. Sil as I had from reading

Professors Sumit Sarkar and Partha Chatterjee on Sri Ramakrishna. In both instances, I have perceptibly differed and deviated from the main line of argument; on the other hand, the dialectical disagreements that I expressed would not have been possible without such brilliant scholars presenting their subjects in a manner that was both evocative and path-breaking.

It has not always been easy to pursue this project. I did not go to the extent of calling Sarada Devi a 'Divine Dowager' as Prof. Sil did, thereby inviting the wrath of the Ramakrishna establishment. However, I could sense from the experiences he reported that my own project too could not hope to win their approval or cooperation. I did try to correspond with the Ramakrishna Sarada Math in Dakshineswar and in New Delhi, but without any success.

I take this occasion to thank friends and colleagues who have inspired and encouraged me through this challenging journey. My friend Jeffery Long, himself an outstanding scholar of the Ramakrishna Vivekananda tradition, strongly backed the idea of writing this biography and it was delightful to exchange mails with the kindly Pravrajika Vrajaprana of Santa Barbara, California. My daughter-in-law, Shrobona, ungrudgingly helped in procuring books, journal articles and unpublished dissertations obtainable through the interlibrary loan of American universities. At most times, this proved critical.

This is the first biography of a woman that I have attempted and predictably, the challenges were great. On the way I have had to negotiate somewhat reductive historians, greatly assertive feminists and pious readings of a life that at times failed to set apart the human face of Sarada Devi from the divine. However, I did not entirely agree with Prof. Sil's allegation that the monk scholars writing on Sarada Devi have thoroughly dehumanized, denatured and thoughtlessly deified their subject. To them must also go the credit of making available to us a substantial body of literature that in effect does quite the opposite. This comprises testimonies from lay devotees and casual acquaintances of Sarada, which carry a wealth of detail and spontaneously evocative personal memories. A good number of these have been obtained from lower-caste manual labourers, like palki-bearers, fisherwoman and domestic workers who came to be associated with the Holy Mother at various times. This is the kind of literature that is conspicuously absent even in the case of Sri Ramakrishna. I take this occasion also to reveal how others too have been similarly misjudged in the past. Scholars have now cast doubt upon the accuracy and authenticity of Mahendranath Gupta's almost stenographic reporting in the *Kathamrita*. Even allowing for lapses, I have to say that Gupta was honest enough to include in his work material that is brutally candid and courageous in its reporting, and whether in his day or thereafter, it would have shocked and scandalized many admirers and devotees of Sri Ramakrishna.

Unlike some feminist scholars I did not think that Sarada Devi was a guru entirely in her own right and that she carved out an independent spiritual path for herself that could be effectively set apart from that laid down by her god-man husband. On the other hand, charisma, on that exalted level, is not always a matter of a distinct religious identity or demonstrated spiritual prowess. It could equally originate in simple and spontaneous feelings of devotion and affect in individuals and groups. A ubiquitous and universal motherhood that her devotees and disciples foisted upon Sarada Devi serves as both cause and effect in explaining much of her charismatic popularity. Feminist critics have, however, alerted me about the ways in which Hindu renunciation is gendered and our pressing need to confer greater social recognition than is presently the case, on the world of female renunciation and female renouncers.

This slim book is not exactly meant for scholars. It seeks only to offer to the interested lay reader an accessible, instructive and enjoyable engagement with a life that calls for greater approbation.

INTRODUCTION

I found nothing supernatural in her. Unlike her husband, Ramakrishna, she did not go into the rapturous state of samadhi every now and then; nor would she deliver some mystical or imperceptible discourses before her devotees in that state. To me it seemed she was no more than an ideal Hindu woman, chaste and immaculately pure, and a typically affectionate mother.

—Swami Ishanananda[1]

The venom in sinful seekers that we ourselves could not digest, we promptly transferred to the care of the Holy Mother... It was she who represented unbridled grace and limitless compassion... I never found Sri Ramakrishna himself to extend his grace so readily or freely... He would accept a disciple only after subjecting him to the most rigorous tests.

—Swami Premananda[2]

In one of his several instructive parables narrated before his devotees, Sri Ramakrishna Paramahamsa

1 My translation.

2 My translation.

(1836–86) compared himself to the grocer who stocked a wide variety of merchandise in keeping with the varying needs of his consumers. With the use of this parable, he intended to convey two related ideas. In the first place, this was meant to suggest the deeply ecumenical nature of his religious ideas, capable of catering to a variety of spiritual seekers, each with his own disposition and requirements. But his intention here was also to convey that there was no inherent conflict in his treading on multiple paths, for atop the difference in methods was foisted a common human objective: God realization. Much the same could be said of his wife, Saradamani Devi (1853–1920) who, in her lifetime and thereafter, was perceived in different ways and yet continued to be the focus of a large but motley community of devotees and admirers. As with her husband, she appeared differently to different groups, but in ways that did not reduce her overall charisma or the inner unity of reverential feeling and affect. She was seen as the head of a spiritual family comprising monks and celibates (*sanghajanani*), but also the nucleus of popular devotion *(lokajanani)*; she was perceived both as an advanced spiritual practitioner, but also the divine object of such praxis herself. She was loved as the quintessential mother figure, respected as the ideal Hindu wife, revered as a saintly ascetic whose life was marked by austerity and self-denial, but also the householder deeply implicated in everyday problems of life and yet negotiating practicable solutions around these. In her lifetime, she was acknowledged as no less than an avatar figure by the first twelve presidents of the Ramakrishna Mission barring the fifth, Swami Subodhananda (1867–1932), who died prematurely within a few months of his nomination as President. In 1920, when she passed away, the number of her devotees and disciples may well have exceeded those of Sri Ramakrishna himself. Sarada Devi was not the biological mother to any children but that may have only contributed towards consolidating her position as the Universal Mother. As a biological mother, she may have been accused of being partial to her own children; not being one ended that possible conflict of choices. Quite naively, as it would now seem, Saradamani refused to see her 'English children' as any different from the Indian, thereby dissolving, in a manner of speaking, all incipient or real political conflict between an alien colonial rule and its rightful opponents.

This brings to the fore an important methodological question regarding a modern reappraisal of the life and times of Sarada Devi. Evidently, there is a case for setting apart self-understanding or subjectivity from that which is framed by contemporary social and historical contexts. Sarada Devi was by no means unaware of the political duress or the economic peril under which Indians had been placed during colonial rule or even of the natural freedom of self-determination being denied to the colonized. And yet, this did not keep her from articulating an idealized construction of a protective, non-discriminating, ubiquitous motherhood that transcended social and political barriers. Perhaps, we could justly use the same methodological argument to rationalize the inherently conflicting public perceptions about her.

In the biographical literature concerning her, it is commonly reported that most people were attracted to Sarada Devi since she somehow reminded them of their own mother. This has encouraged scholars to believe that what was essentially at play here was the fulfilment of some emotional and psychological need. Contemporary scholars like the historian Narasingha P. Sil have also highlighted the cultural context to such occurrences. Hindu Bengalis, we are given to understand, were particularly apt to reveal a child-like reversion to the mother figure as a matter of cultural habit. On the other hand, the relationship between collective culture and individual psychology can often be skewed. For instance, we cannot be sure if cultural postulates induce certain patterns of psychological behavior or if psychology itself feeds on entrenched cultural idioms. There is a complex alignment between the two, which is only apt to acknowledge. Thus, the psychological phenomena of a child-like reversion before a human mother figure may well find its wings in shared religious norms too. It cannot be a coincidence, after all, that Sarada Devi's emergence as the quintessential mother occurred at a time when a renewed emphasis was placed on the concept of 'motherhood of God'. Incidentally, this had been articulated not by contemporary Hindu saints as Ramakrishna alone, but also iconoclastic Brahmos like Keshab Chandra Sen. It occurs to me, therefore, that in the case of Sarada Devi, the two faces of the 'mother', human and the divine, overlapped, blurred or else were deliberately conflated.

The Quintessential Mother

In present day West Bengal, Jairambati, the birth place of Saradamani, is one of the principal sites of religious tourism. It is a site that people visit with feelings of unconcealed reverence, joyously accept food offerings (*prasada*), collect photographic souvenirs and other memorabilia and return home apparently with a sense of fulfilment. The aura of the place is indisputably religious and cultic; it is a site frequented by the young and old alike, by men and women carrying an air of expectation, seeking the benediction of one not simply an ordinary mortal but a luminal figure placed between time and immortality. It is very likely that Jairambati is a spot where housewives privately renew their marital vows before the woman who was herself a most doting and devoted wife to her husband and where widows seek forbearance and ways to soften the burden of widowhood. But such vows, I imagine, are also tied to notions of acquiring religious merit (*punya*) that accrue from the wife's or widow's life-long fidelity to the spouse. Arguably, men too may find it easier to relate as a child to a mother figure who is not a biological mother. Biological mothers are compelled to lead social lives which, as human experiences, are not always pleasant or palatable. Divinity turns more tangible when divorced from the existential pangs of everyday relationships. At Jairambati, people revere the Holy Mother because her holiness comes also from transcending mundane experiences.

A reading of Sarada's much-acclaimed motherhood purely along psychological lines will not work for another reason. In substance, the epithet 'Holy Mother' was as much the creation of Sarada Devi herself as of her admiring devotees. Saradamani fully believed in her divine character or antecedents and a part of this was born of self-understanding. For one, she was fully aware of the great spiritual standing of her god-man husband, of his growing popularity in the bhadralok society of colonial Calcutta and the interest that his life and teachings had begun to generate even outside India. She considered herself to be the rightful *sahadharmini*, Sri Ramakrishna's partner in spiritual life, and her husband entrusting her to carry on with his mission after him would have presumably held much meaning for her. She may not have been Sri Ramakrishna's 'first and foremost disciple' as is sometimes claimed in hagiography, but as his spouse she nevertheless enjoyed a position that could not have been rivalled by any of the Master's male or female disciples. Even without undergoing a rigorous spiritual regimen herself or working out impressive miracles, she had to be the natural spiritual heir to her husband. Here, it would be important to recall too that especially after the death of Sri Ramakrishna, palpable differences surfaced between some of his direct disciples over interpreting his life and words. Swamis Premananda (1861–1918) and Yogananda (1861–99) were two (among possibly more) individuals who doubted some of Swami Vivekananda's (1863–1902) interpretations of the Master's teachings. For one, they were unhappy at Vivekananda's objections to bestowing avatar status on Ramakrishna, especially before Western devotees and the press. Possibly, they were also among those displeased to hear reports of Vivekananda's consuming 'un-Hindu' food in America. At the Belur Math itself, some monks considered it outlandish that they be awakened every morning by the punctual ringing of the alarm clock as Vivekananda reportedly arranged. It is important also not to overlook how Sarada Devi herself considered 'Naren' (Vivekananda) to be but an instrument in the hands of his guru, destined to perform tasks as his Master had planned for him. The key to his favourite pupil's life and work lay in the hands of his guru, she consistently claimed. Given the potential crisis in leadership within the monastic organization, Sarada's ascent to the position of the cult leader is really no cause for surprise. Traditionally, the wife of a guru (*gurupatni*) was a natural choice as his successor within a spiritual organization but that apart, she was also the *guru ma*, the female guru who held the status of a mother. I am inclined to think that herein lies part of the explanation behind Sarada Devi's rise to the position of at least the *sanghajanani.* I feel also that her undisputed and unflagging devotion to her husband, even to the point of elevating him to the status of *ishtadevata* (the coveted personal deity) proved to be more than a mere wifely sentiment for her followers. It had deeper cultural meaning, confirming in some ways traditionally prescriptive roles to be performed by the ideal Hindu woman and wife in relation to the husband who was deemed to be her superior in every respect. Not surprisingly, Swami Abhedananda (1866–1939), the first among the monks of the Ramakrishna Order to compose Sanskrit *stotras* in praise of the Holy Mother, described her as 'pativrata swarupini' (the embodiment of marital faithfulness). I would be willing to argue that such fidelity may also have been construed as the source of ritual purity and holiness.

Situating Sarada Devi

It is relatively easier to determine what Sarada Devi was not, than what she actually was. She was certainly not an ascetic or saint in the accepted sense of these terms, not even a *brahmacharini* or the celibate woman who had been formally initiated by a guru to that office. Her peculiar social or spiritual status is better understood against the backdrop of traditional Hindu-brahmanical notions of world renunciation. Renunciation in this tradition, it has to be admitted, was visibly gendered. Women were held capable of reaching a high state of spiritual consciousness, but this did not necessarily qualify them for attaining the status of a *sanyasini.* The underlying paradox here is rather telling. On the one hand, women were taken to possess certain qualities more amenable to the spirit of renunciation, as for instance, their natural penchant for the selfless acts of giving, feeding or nurturing. On the other hand, these very qualities inhibited their entry into the world of *sanyas,* for such roles also implicated them in everyday lives and suggested that the woman's salvation lay more in fulfilling her household duties. This was her natural dharma (*stridharma*) whereby fulfilling her duties of a wife or mother was tantamount to attaining *moksha.* There is a subtle but important distinction that the Hindu tradition also makes between the woman ascetic and the ascetic widow. The woman ascetic is not required to follow *stridharma*; the widow, though following an ascetic lifestyle, certainly is. Apart from especially carrying on with routine household duties, the widow was also expected to fall in line with qualities specifically required of her (*vaidhabya dharma*). Cases of women joining *sanyas* are not unknown, but it is also obvious that the more ritualistic acts underlying the process of accepting *sanyas* do not always apply to them. Even as a *grihi* or householder, the woman was not ordinarily permitted the performance of either funeral rites (*sradh*) or the annual ritual remembrance of ancestors (*tarpan*). The word 'sadhu' has really no feminine parallel in the Hindu religious lexicon since the term *sadhvi,* used commonly, is at best ambiguous. It may mean both the female sadhu, but also the chaste Hindu wife.[3] In the

3 It is interesting though that the tradition of non-dualist Vedanta (Advaita), which is generally taken to be socially conservative and has traditionally denied women access to esoteric texts *(shruti)*, accepted the idea of women taking to *sanyas* before the relatively less conservative orders like the Madhva sampradaya. The Ramakrishna Order, though formally affiliated to the non-dualist lineage would also have to be one of the earliest to join social service to the spiritual praxis in the life of its monks. Its declared motto is *atmanam mokshartha, jagat hitaya cha* (liberation for the self and service to the world). The varied responses to the question of accepting women as ascetics among monastic orders have been empirically studied in T.S. Rukmani's: *Sanyasin in the Hindu Tradition (Changing Perspectives)*, printed by D.K. Print World, Delhi, 2011.

present day, media-savvy female gurus are not hard to come by; on the other hand, some Hindu religious organizations, historically noted for their willingness to recruit women and now with an international presence, have still not developed the idea of a female guru. The ISCKON still does not have one.[4]

It occurs to me that Saradamani was aware of the complex position in which contemporary history and society had placed her. Recent anthropological research has demonstrated that even those women who take to the spirit of *bairagya* (renunciation and detachment) do still prefer to retain a sense of their femininity. It is my surmise that Sarada Devi did just that in two related ways: first, by concentrating on her routine household duties and second, by arrogating to herself the role of an all-knowing, all-caring, universal mother. After all, motherhood, whether real or imagined, did transmit the nurturing, protecting and fecund quality of femininity. Sarada Devi's dedicated and diligent focus on household work in the capacity of a housekeeper and mother figure

4 Even in the 1940s, women ascetics were writing on the Hindu woman's natural right to *sanyas*. One such work was by Asha Debi—*Pravrajika Muktiprana: Sanyase Hindu Narir Adhikar*, 1946. The author was the first General Secretary of the Sarada Math, the female wing of the Ramakrishna Order.

was noticed by some observant contemporaries. The Brahmo preacher, Protapchandra Mozumdar (1856–1912), was to write thus:

> Safe or unsafe, girl or grandmother, she preached all her life an utter self-devotion to the household outside of which she recognized no obligation.[5]

Saradamani in Biographical Literature: Pious, Pedantic and Profane

A good part of our understanding of Sarada Devi springs from the way she has been studied and projected in contemporary literature and in more recent academic studies. In hindsight, it has to be admitted that in the case of both Sri Ramakrishna and his wife, Saradamani, it was the Brahmo press which first took note of them. On Ramakrishna, there were several press notices between 1875 and 1879 appearing in the *Indian Mirror*, *Dharmatattwa* and the *Theistic Quarterly Review*. The last of these was by none other than Protapchandra Mozumdar who, as we

5 P.C. Mozumdar, "The Emancipation of Women in Bengal" in *The Calcutta Review*, April 1904, pp. 125–31.

know, took a keen interest in Sarada Devi's life. As is now well known, Mozumdar, writing to Max Muller, had complained of Ramakrishna's cruel treatment of his wife, relegated allegedly to a life of neglect and denied the natural pleasures of a conjugal life. About seven years after Sarada Devi's passing away, there also appeared in the popular journal *Prabasi,* edited by another Brahmo luminary, Ramananda Chatterjee (1865–1943), a biographical sketch of Sarada Devi, the first of its kind, if we are to overlook short and inconsequential obituary notices that appeared in the journals run by the Ramakrishna Order: *Udbodhan*, *Prabuddha Bharata* and *Vedanta Kesari* between July and November, 1920.[6] Chatterjee followed up with an English version of the *Prabasi* article in *The Modern Review* of June 1927, also edited by him. The *Prabasi* article pointedly argued that the life of Sarada Devi was much too important to lie banished within the domain of sectarian hagiography coming from her numerous devotees and disciples. She deserved a more objective and professional treatment, Chatterjee pleaded. It took over a decade for another writer, also impressed with the life of the Holy Mother, to reiterate this view.

6 For more details see the Bibliography appended to this work.

This work, authored by Naliniranjan Chattopadhyay,[7] appeared in the year 1959 and claimed to strictly follow a historical chronology in evaluating the life and times of Sarada Devi. The book was among the earliest to include the teachings of Sarada as were publicly known at that stage. Most importantly, Chattopadhyay took serious note of Ramananda Chatterjee's appeal for producing a professionally competent biography of the Holy Mother.

For a long time, the biographical literature on Sarada Devi was unquestionably dominated by contributions from monk biographers of the Ramakrishna Order. They did not encourage even lay devotees to write for the fear that outside the definitional periphery set by themselves, the life of the Holy Mother may be misconstrued or seriously misinterpreted.[8] That it was not easy to understand or interpret the charisma of the Mother was an idea that appears to have taken hold of men even in Saradamani's lifetime.

---

7 From *Sri Sri Ma Sarada: Kalanulkramik Jeebon o Kathamrita.* Chattopadhyay also authored a valuable monograph on Ramakrishna's patronage of the Bengali stage. See his *Sri Ramakrishna O Banga Rangamancha*. Calcutta, 1978.

8 Swami Saradananda's so discouraging a potential biographer by the name of Labanyakumar Chakrabarti is a well-known instance.

The literature produced by the monk-scholars comprises broadly two genres of writings. First, there are full-length biographies in Bengali and English, and second, memoirs, anecdotes and reminiscences authored by lay devotees and monks. The latter variety has been exclusively compiled and edited by monks and marketed by the publishing wings of the Ramakrishna Mission. This would have helped, one imagines, not only to generate generous revenue from book sales, but also extend some degree of control over what was made public. Each of these collections has undergone successive reprints.

Full-length biographies of Sarada Devi appear to have arrived in two identifiable clusters, the first dating back to the period between the 1930s and 1960s and the second, produced in the 1980s and thereafter. The first full-length biography of Sarada Devi, written in Bengali and authored by a novitiate attached to the Ramakrishna Math and Mission, Brahmachari Akshaychaitanya, appeared in 1937. Akshaychaitanya has also rendered valuable service by providing us biographical sketches of other monks of the Ramakrishna Order—as for instance, Swami Premananda, but more importantly for our purposes, an inventory of names of Sarada's devotees and disciples as could be collected up to about the mid 1940s.[9] This is an amazingly rich document of a kind which was never attempted in respect of the followers of Sri Ramakrishna himself. Between 1940 and 1961, at least six full-length biographies were published by prominent monks of the Ramakrishna Order, each of them holding responsible positions within the Ramakrishna organization in India and abroad. The list includes swamis Tapasyananda, Pavitrananda, Gambhirananda and Nikhilananda. Two of these were published from Ramakrishna Math, Mylapore. Gambhirananda, the 11th president of the Order and the official historian of the Ramakrishna Math and Mission, first produced a Bengali biography in 1954, coinciding with Sarada Devi's birth centenary celebrations, and followed this up with an English version in 1977. His studies are, by all appearances, the most theologized when it comes to interpreting the life of Sarada. Nikhilananda's biography was first published from the USA with financial support from an American devotee, Chester F. Carlston. The Indian edition followed a year later, in 1962. Nikhilananda (pre-monastic name: Dineshchandra Dasgupta), once

9 For a brief analysis of this list, see "Sarada Devi: A Reappraisal".

a political detainee, was a direct disciple of Sarada Devi. For his book, he admits to have relied heavily on the work of a lay devotee, Mandasankar Dasgupta, originally published in 1956, but with several reprints since. Parts of this book he admits to have translated in the course of his sermons before his students and disciples at the Thousand Island Park in New York, where Swami Vivekananda himself had once camped. Within the first cluster of biographies, we may also include two other prominent works, one of them by the celebrity author, Achintyakumar Sengupta,[10] and the other by a lay devotee of Sarada Devi by the name of Ashutosh Mitra who eventually left the Ramakrishna Order. A third biography written during this period was by Durgapuri Devi who was, in all probability, a member of the Saradeswari Ashram, begun by one of Sarada's close companions, Gauri Ma (Mridani Chattopadhyay, 1857–1938).

In the period beginning with the 1980s, relatively shorter biographies were produced by swamis Bhumananda, Ishanananda, Purnatmananda, Sri Arcanapuri and Pravrajika Muktiprana.

10 Sengupta is equally famed for his multivolume biography of Ramakrishna, *Paramapurusha Sri Sri Ramakrishna*.

The literature on Sarada Devi has been considerably enriched by first-hand accounts authored by lay devotees and other casual acquaintances. The earliest albeit somewhat scattered reminiscences of Sarada appear in Sister Nivedita's classic, *The Master as I saw Him* (1910), which has fascinating material both on Vivekananda and the Holy Mother. Nivedita, as we know, first met the Mother in 1898 and came to reside in the same locality in north Calcutta as did Sarada Devi herself for some time. She was a prolific writer and correspondent, and her day-to-day impressions of the Holy Mother appear with some regularity in the letters she wrote to her several European and American friends. The first major Bengali collection of reminiscences on Sarada appeared in *Udbodhan* and were later compiled in a very useful two volume set called *Sri Sri Mayer Kotha* by Swami Arupananda. The first of these volumes, published in 1926, had 19 personal accounts of varying lengths, including two of the earliest, authored by Ramananda Chatterjee (to which I have referred earlier) and by Saralabala Sarkar (1875–1961), a great admirer of Nivedita. Interestingly enough, most of these accounts were anonymous, though some clearly belonged to women authors. The anonymity in these early accounts is a little perplexing especially given the detailed identities disclosed by later devotees. The second volume of this work was published over a decade later in 1937. Of the 24 accounts included in this volume, as many as nine were by women devotees and seven by Ramakrishna monks. Select pieces from the two volumes (about 38 in all) were later translated into English by the Ramakrishna Math, Madras, as *Gospel of the Holy Mother: Recorded by her Devotee Children* (1984). Three other comparable collections surfaced soon. The first of these was published by the Udbodhan Press in 1954, again on the occasion of the Holy Mother's centenary celebrations. Of the 84 entries in this volume comprising essays, letters and poems, only about half of them were directly on Sarada Devi herself and presumably, the idea here was to place her in the backdrop of Indian history and culture, to be counted among notable Indian women of all ages. The strategy adopted here closely follows the Sarada centenary volume titled *Great Women of India,* edited by Swami Madhavananda and the historian Ramesh Chandra Majumdar. This was followed by the compilation edited by Swami Hiranmayananda in 1984, put together from articles originally appearing in *Vedanta Kesari* (between 1948 and 1954) and *Prabuddha Bharata* (between 1968 and 1970). The space given to testimonies originating in monks was disproportionately high; in excess of 180 pages for a book that runs into about 460 pages in all. A particular section of this book listed responses from Western women devotees alone. This idea was followed up more recently in Swami Ganeshananda's "How the Holy Mother Influences her Western Devotees".[11] Another highly useful set of four volumes (*Sri Sri Mayer Padaprante*) edited and compiled by Swami Purnatmananda carrying reprints from about half a dozen journals was published between 1994 and 2003. An English version of this work called *Reminscences of Sarada Devi by Monks, Devotees and Others* comprising 28 select testimonies has since been published. In 1997, Swami Purnatmananda edited another useful volume titled *Yugajanani Sarada*, which includes a rare article on photographs taken of the Holy Mother and a detailed chronology prepared by Renuka Chattopadhyay. Many of the reminiscences mentioned above also made their way into the gigantic compilation edited by Swami Lokeswarananda titled *Shatarupe Sarada* (1984).

A work comparable in design and content to *Great Women of India* was *Great Women Saints of East*

11 *Prabuddha Bharata*, 89 (December, 1984) pp. 491–97.

and West edited by Swami Ghanananda and Stewart Wallace (1955). An earlier but little-known work by Rajendralal Acharya, *Banglar Dharmaguru*, including a short sketch of the life and teachings of Sarada Devi, appeared in 1947. The last, I have to admit, I discovered quite accidentally.

Critical accounts of the life and work of Sarada Devi are limited to the researches of the historian Narasingha P. Sil. To date, these have appeared in two forms; a 1998 article published in the online journal, *Asian Journal of Woman's Studies*, followed by a full-length monograph in 2003.

A debate buried not too deeply in Sarada literature is the one between pious readings of her life and the profane. Narasingh P. Sil's work is deliberately framed as a corrective to the way writings from monk scholars have allegedly dehumanized, deified and denatured a simple, unpretentious but intelligent woman, who did find her own ways of self-assertion. Sil's declared mission in his very persuasively argued book is to restore to Sarada Devi the commonplace humanity that is rightfully hers.

In this perception, Sarada Devi is seen to resist, albeit not very successfully, the machinations of her whimsical god-man husband, the patriarchal dictates of her society and the influential body of Ramakrishna monks who purposively cast her in a certain mould. Sil's writings, albeit a tad reductive at places, does help in setting the balance right somewhat, rescuing Sarada from the burden of rather tendentious readings and opening up the possibility of more objective reappraisals.

Sil also shares with feminist writings the tendency to reassess Sarada Devi in the light of modern movements to secure greater space for women. Feminist writings on Sarada precede those of Narasingha Sil by over five decades and, judging by some unpublished dissertations that I have had the good fortune of consulting, they continue to be provocatively productive to this day. The earliest specimens of these writings on Sarada appeared way back in 1953–54 and projected her as a modern woman in every sense of the term who seriously contributed to self-awareness among Indian women.[12]

12 See for instance: Belarani De's "Nari Pragati O Sri Ma" in *Ananda Bazar Patrika*, dated 27.12.1953, and Urmila Chattopadhyay's "Adarsha Nari Sri Sarada Devi" in *Biswabani*, dated 15.12.1360 BS (January 1954). The latest in the line of such productions is Susmita De's *Banglar Nari Mukti Andolan Ebong Sri Sri Ma* (1999).

Both Sil and feminist writers dispute the idea of Saradamani being merely a spiritual helpmate in relation to Ramakrishna. Their position, rather, is that she was capable of advanced spiritual practices and a guru in her own right who could chalk out an independent path for herself. This is sometimes supported by representation made by the male monks of the Ramakrishna Order itself. Some of them have gone on record stating how Sarada Devi was less choosy or discriminating about just whom to accept as a devotee or disciple. There is also no evidence to suggest that Ramakrishna's devotees and disciples went beyond the class of the suburban Bengali bhadralok. His grace rarely seems to have extended to the rural poor, manual labourers, Muslims or the ritually marginalized. On the contrary, in the case of Sarada Devi, these classes constituted a substantial part of the entourage and thanks to some painstaking research carried out by monk-scholars themselves, several people belonging to these categories can now be identified by name, occupation and residence. Some of these accounts represent the most personalized and emotionally drawn profiles of the Holy Mother at the peak of her fame. Further down this book I have demonstrated how it was rarely that the Holy Mother refused to initiate a spiritual seeker even though she was, at times, visibly disturbed at the prospect of having to deal with those particularly difficult or undeserving.

The problem with some feminist scholars though is that while they take Sarada Devi to be capable of advanced spiritual practices, they fail to drive the argument to its hilt. Thus, the scholar Trishia Nicole Goulet, whom I often cite in the course of this study, argues that the purity and holiness in Sarada Devi originated not so much in her spiritual practices as in the unconsummated marriage.[13] On one level, this acknowledges the fact that the Holy Mother cannot be identified with a coherent religious discourse and much of her logia represent a commonsensical and ethical view of matters rather than the doctrinal or the philosophical. Sometime in 1901, when she supported Vivekananda in determining that the followers of Ramakrishna had to be *advaitin*s since their guru himself was one, she could not have been speaking from any acutely philosophical understanding of either

13 Trishia Nicole Goulet, "The Lives of Sarada Devi: Gender, Renunciation and Hindu Politics in Colonial India" (Unpublished PhD thesis, Department of Religion, University of Manitoba, Winnipeg, 2009).

advaita or Sri Ramakrishna's own understanding of it. Also, it is a somewhat synthetic wedge that Goulet drives between holiness and continence and purity born of continence and that arising in spiritual practices. Continence, as I have argued could be a source of *tapas* or spiritual energy. I have some reservations too about the argument advanced by both Goulet and Sil to the effect that the life and work of Sarada Devi represents an important dimension of women's struggle for identity in colonial India. This is the view with which our monk-scholars would agree, but from an opposite end. From their perspective, Sarada Devi was undoubtedly modern inasmuch as she stood up for the just treatment of women, advocated female education and did not take marriage to be mandated for girls in every case. But from this perspective, women's emancipation was also to be bounded by certain limits. Sarada Devi encouraged women to stand up for themselves, they aver, but not at the cost of overrunning established social values and conventions. The modernization that the Holy Mother approved of would have still seen the Indian woman as Indian and with a spiritual angst vitally defining and determining her profile. For Swami Nikhilananda, Sarada Devi represents the ideal Indian woman of all ages, ranging from the mythical Sita or Savitri to the modern day professional. His point really is that the Holy Mother belongs to all ages and all cultures, regardless of changes in social and historical contexts. Swami Mumukshananda finds her life to be a useful corrective to brazenly debunking the spiritual in the name of woman's progress. Swami Gambhirananda feels that while Indian women ought to be woken up from their quiescence and energized in the manner of their Western counterpart, this cannot be done at the expense of the timeless Indian ideals of spirituality. Even back in the 1940s, Swami Tapasyananda had warned the Indian woman not to lose her soul by way of mimicking the male.

The struggle waged by women for a new identity and greater space in a modern environment is historically tied to a class with which Sarada Devi had only tenuous links. Though a Brahmin in terms of caste standing, she did not quite belong to the category of the *bhadramahila* (female counterpart of the bhadralok) which, in the context of colonial Bengal, was the class largely implicated in socially transformative campaigns. Her marriage to Sri Ramakrishna would have added to her acceptability in the urban society of late-19th-century Calcutta and in time further enhanced through her acquaintance with Vivekananda's foreign disciples. Sarada Devi did create a niche for herself and she was by no means a passive conformist in matters of everyday social and cultural life. Without a doubt, she influenced some women educators and activists like Nivedita, Sister Sudhira or Pravrajika Bharatiprana, but this, I feel, was more a matter of charisma—the very simplicity and nobility of her personal example, than some carefully framed reformist discourse.

It is this unassuming simplicity coupled with an endearing tenderness of feeling that largely explains the popularity she enjoyed. Her very presence encouraged a childlike surrender before one who could effectively alternate between a compassionate mother figure and the benignly divine or perhaps even combine the two. Comparing even the comparables is bound to have its limits but here I cannot but think of a comparison, however superficial that may prove to be, between Saradamani and an equally celebrated female spiritual figure from Bengal who also long enjoyed ascriptions of motherhood, Anandamayi Ma (Nirmala Sundari Chakrabarty, 1896–1982). Sarada Devi did not have the wit or the spiritual repertoire of Anandamayi Ma[14] and unlike her younger contemporary again, she would not understand spiritual ecstasy as *kheyal* (moods). Sarada Devi was not as keen to be photographed as was Anandamayi Ma and certainly not in ecstatic moods or postures. On the other hand, there is something unobtrusively commonplace about her which catches the eye every time one views her.

14 Ananadamayi Ma once interpreted Vedanta (the end of the Vedas or else its essence) as 'bhedanta' (bhed+anta), i.e., the end of all distinction or differentiation!

EARLY LIFE, MARRIAGE AND DAYS AT DAKSHINESWAR

Sarada Devi was born on 22 December 1853, to poor Brahmin parents, Ramchandra Mukhopadhyay and Shyamasundari Devi, of the village Jairambati, district Bankura, West Bengal. Interestingly enough, she underwent a successive change of names in early childhood. Originally called Khemankari (the auspicious) she was subsequently given the names Saradasundari and Saradamani. The last name stuck, but was shortened to Sarada in popular usage. Much significance was later attached to this name since in the perception of some, her god-man husband Ramakrishna's included, this invoked Saraswati, the Hindu goddess of learning. Outside hagiographic readings of her life, this is nothing short of a startling paradox since Sarada was less literate than even her husband Ramakrishna, who could sign his name and at best write a few words in legible Bengali. There is reason to believe that she was herself keen to learn, but actively discouraged by some close relatives. Hriday Mukhopadhyay, Ramakrishna's nephew would not allow her to pursue the study of *Barnaparichay*, the Bengali primer popularized by the educationist Iswarchandra Vidyasagar (1820–91) for fear that this would divest Sarada of her womanly nature or qualities. As a young adult, she did briefly return to develop some basic literacy skills. Sister Nivedita (1867–1911), Swami Vivekananda's foremost disciple, tells us that she could read aloud the (Bengali) *Ramayana* of Krittibas Ojha but was unable to carry out her own correspondence. That was handled either by her nieces or young monks of the Ramakrishna Order who served her in various capacities.

Saradamani was the eldest of several children born to the couple and this placed her in a position of great responsibility when it came to suitably bringing up her siblings. In all, she had five brothers and a sister. Of these, the sister Kadambini and second brother, Umesh, died in infancy. The youngest of her brothers, Abhayacharan, died shortly after he had qualified for a medical degree. Abhay's widow, Surabala, who suffered mental derangement following her husband's untimely death, was to play an important role in Sarada's life. Her erratic and at times unpredictably violent behaviour caused considerable anxiety and irritation to all family members. Their only daughter, Radharani, popularly called Radhu, proved to be even a greater source of anxiety and developed signs of mental derangement herself. Sarada Devi was greatly attached to this niece for nearly all of her adult life only to dramatically sever her bonds shortly before her own death in 1920. She was also a victim of recurring family squabbles, especially between her brothers who constantly fought over their share in ancestral property. Radhu herself and her cousins, Sushila (more commonly known as Maku) and Nalini, daughters of Sarada's eldest brother, Prasannakumar, had unhappy married lives and showed great reluctance to live together with their in-laws. Both Maku and Radhu also lost their infant children to fatal diseases, events that caused acute distress and depression from which they never fully recovered. Forced to constantly witness and to intercede in such disturbing and unpleasant occurrences, Sarada naturally gave many disciples and casual visitors the impression of being almost inextricably involved in mundane, everyday matters. Some even suspected that this occurred at the expense of her own spiritual life. There was, however, an edifying and instructive side to such traumatic experiences. Drawn fairly early and repeatedly into such everyday problems affecting her larger household, Sarada used her gathering experiences to certain constructive ends. Arguably, the caring, mediating, protectively affectionate and motherly qualities that she later exhibited in life towards devotees and disciples had roots in such early experiences.

The Mukhopadhyays were one of the two oldest Brahmin families to be settled in village Jairambati. In 1076 CE reportedly, one Khelatram Mukhopadhyay who served as a priest to the folk deity, Dharma, was granted 17 *kotha*s of rent-free land by Chaitanya Singh Deb of the Vishnupur Raj. Prima facie, royal patronage of a Brahmin priest for Dharma appears to be interesting since we do know that this role was subsequently appropriated by Doms and Bagdis (mostly scavengers and manual workers considered 'ritually defiled') who patronized the Dharma cult. These castes were rebelliously anti-Brahmin, but they still preferred not to abolish the office of the priest. By the 17th century, the Vishnupur Raj itself had turned into a major patron of Gaudiya or Bengal Vaishnavism, moving away from its association with the worship of local folk deities. It is an interesting coincidence too that both Sri Ramakrishna's father, Khudiram Chattopadhyay, and Sarada's father, Ramchandra Mukhopadhyay, were poor but upright Brahmins. Both, incidentally, were also devotees of Rama, although they worshipped other local deities too. It is interesting too to note how they came to look upon the identity of Lord Rama. Khudiram, for instance, was known to make regular offerings of *khichuri*, a common dish prepared by mixing rice and lentils in a given proportion. Reportedly, he went by the impression that this would better suit the palate of a deity whose 'origins' lay in north India! Though poor, both preferred to lead honourable and dignified lives as befitting a high-caste Brahmin. Khudiram spurned gifts from affluent low-caste patrons and Ramchandra was a generous man who would habitually invite home travellers passing by for a smoke or a humble snack. Going by Sarada's own recollections, her father, who had very little property himself, ran a free kitchen for successive days during the devastating famine of 1864 which had badly affected district Bankura. Even in her adult life, she would recall with horror the traumatic experiences she had of feeding utterly famished people who simply could not wait for the hot gruel to cool before gulping it down hurriedly. Some, as she recollected, even chewed on the leaf plate on which food had been served. However, Ramchandra died early, with his sons still in their early childhood, leaving Shyamasundari to eke out a very modest living thereafter. The poor widow toiled hard, husking paddy for her richer neighbours in return for a small portion of the husked paddy. She also used locally grown cotton to prepare the sacred thread habitually worn by Brahmins. Jairambati itself had very few Brahmin households and apparently, her patrons had to be spread over adjacent villages. Shyamasundari consistently suffered from a frail health and prolonged illness. Poverty combined with ill health prevented her from bringing up all her children by herself; three of her sons had to be hosted by close relatives in neighbouring villages. A very young Sarada, by then already married, had to regularly assist her father in cooking and daily household chores. However, her tender age also placed certain practical limits on herself. For instance, at meal time, though able to set the rice boiling in large pots, she lacked the strength to take them off the fire when the rice was cooked and ready. That task had to be carried out by Ramchandra himself. Both Shyamasundari and Sarada were ardent, hard-working and disciplined housekeepers. Even as a young child, Sarada was known to assist her family with other routine duties as for instance, carrying the midday meal to casual workers labouring in the paddy fields, gather fodder for the cattle, sometimes in knee-deep water and collect what was left of a paddy crop after severe locust attacks. All her life, she retained a good sense of just what kind of treatment suited whom and how people could be best handled in keeping with their varying dispositions or requirements. This is reminiscent of the very evocative parable that Sri Ramakrishna often narrated before his disciples of the all-knowing mother who knew just what kind of cooking best suited each of her children. After she was married, a good part of such instructions came from Ramakrishna himself who was keen to ensure that his wife could turn out to be a good housekeeper and understood the domestic economy of the Hindus in its vital details and ran it as efficiently and economically as possible.

Family fortunes of the Mukhopadhyays marginally improved when the eldest son Prasannakumar found employment as a priest in a Calcutta household. This has a striking resemblance again to the life and career of Sri Ramakrishna's elder brother, Ramkumar Chattopadhyay, who initially ran a *tol* in north Calcutta, but later assumed the duties of a priest at Rani Rasmoni's temple complex at Dakshineswar. In mid-19th-century Calcutta, apparently, there had come up a new crop of aspiring nouveau riche drawn from the intermediary and lower castes, who used a conformist and orthodox lifestyle to enhance their social standing. Some such families insisted on employing Brahmin cooks and Ramchandra's younger brother, Nilmadhav too served the well-known Paikpara zamindars in north Calcutta in the capacity of a cook. The man never married and by the time he returned to his village, he had clearly saved enough to avoid having to depend on the charity of a friend or relative. Sarada herself volunteered to take good care of this aged uncle and spoke unhappily of how women from a younger generation had almost entirely forsaken such social and family responsibilities.

Jairambati is located at the south-west corner of district Bankura, its northern border being framed by the local river, Amodar. For local inhabitants and especially for Saradamani herself, the Amodar was comparable to the holy Ganga itself. For all her life, Sarada preferred living close to a water body or a river; living for a time at Bagbazar in north Calcutta and at Belur (district Howrah), both sites in close vicinity of the Ganga, was an emotionally fulfilling experience for her. Jairambati was encircled by some fairly populous villages like Tejpur, Jibta, Kayapat and Sihor, each at about a mile's distance from each other. Sihor was the residence of Saradamani's maternal uncle and one of Ramakrishna's two sisters, possibly Sarvamangala. It is not improbable, therefore, that Sarada's marriage to Ramakrishna in 1859 was facilitated by the two families having known each other, however distantly. Such probabilities, however, are discounted by hagiographers since the commonly accepted version today is that both Sri Ramakrishna and Sarada clearly foretold their choice of partner. Further down this chapter, we shall see how Ramakrishna foretold his marriage to Sarada and there is a similar story to the effect that even an infant Sarada pointed to her would-be husband amidst a large group of men and women who had gathered for a religious festival.

Sihor was famous also for annual celebrations, popularly known as 'gajan' and associated with the god, Shiva. It was also a prosperous trading site in the area housing the main grocery shops. In Saradamani's lifetime, Jairambati itself was a less populated village of about a hundred households only. The majority of its population was drawn from the Bagdis and Doms, Kaivartas (petty peasants and fishermen), Dules (palki bearers), Goalas (milkmen) and Kayasthas (an intermediary caste ritually placed just below the Brahmins). The village did not grow enough food locally and had to depend on supplies transported by vendors from adjoining villages. In the generation preceding Sarada's, the adjacent villages of Shiromanipur and Paramanandapur had also seen a thriving business of mulberry cultivation, mostly run by local Muslims. After the East India Company's mercantilist policy began to negatively affect the local production of silk threads and cloth, many of the silk workers who lost their employment turned to looting and brigandage. One such character was Amjad, of whom we shall hear more. Jairambati was, however, made famous on account of some important religious icons and shrines located in the area. It can be no coincidence that the village was best known for its distinctive tortoise-shaped Dharma icons called Jatrasiddhi Ray and Suryanarayan. An additional attraction was the Singhabahini (literally, the goddess mounted on the lion) temple which assumed far greater importance once Sarada Devi's name came to be associated with it. When sufficiently appeased, the Goddess was known to cure troublesome and malignant diseases. Sarada Devi herself persistently suffered from dysentery, at times in acute forms, and the extant biographies reveal that she always carried on her person a small tin box containing the holy dust gathered around the Singhabahini complex. A pinch of that dust she would trustingly consume each time she developed pain and discomfort. Jairambati was once also known for its annual Kali Puja festival, but this was discontinued following differences between the two oldest and most influential Brahmin families in the village: the Mukhopadhyays and the Bandopadhyays. Reportedly, the latter were the more affluent of the two and allegedly, they used some clever ruse to deny their rivals participation in the Kali Puja festivities. In the long run though, this created new opportunities for the Mukhopadhyay family, for legend has it that a greatly distressed Shyamasundari Devi was once visited by no less than Goddess Jagaddhatri (literally, the keeper of the world), a form of the Great Mother, who acceded to an annual worship being held in her honour. Saradamani inherited this tradition from her mother. Later in life, even when stationed at distant Belur or else in Calcutta, she made every effort to visit Jairambati in November each year, specifically with the intention of organizing the annual Jagaddhatri puja. This she could not do with any regularity, since certain material considerations came in the way. For one, her brothers did not always cooperate financially or otherwise. The second brother, Kalikumar, insisted on taking charge of all the necessary purchases for the puja, an opportunity he then used to siphon off some money for himself. Petty village rivalries too came in the way and at times, Saradamani had to put up with some indifference and hostility from her neighbours, especially from those who remained circumspect about her claims to spiritual fame and eyed with some suspicion her continuing association with young male monks of the Ramakrishna Order. Even Prasannakumar, who hosted Saradamani whenever she visited her ancestral home, was discomfited by the ever-swelling number of disciples and devotees pouring into Jairambati with the intention of seeking her blessings and benedictions. Prasannakumar found this to be a nuisance and an encroachment on family property which potentially carried some risks. None of Sarada's brothers showed any interest in the spiritual discourse preached by the Ramakrishna Order or agreed to be initiated by any of the monks or even by their own sister at the height of her spiritual fame. Kalikumar Mukhopadhyay even disputed Sarada's 'divine' status. On one level, this is ironical, since it was Swami Saradananda (1865–1927), a direct disciple of Ramakrishna who helped arrive at an amicable settlement regarding shares in the family property between the perpetually warring brothers. As matters eventually turned out, Saradamani had the astuteness to forewarn her brothers that unless they exacted their share of the ancestral property on time, they might soon lose the property itself to thronging devotees who wished to convert it into a public shrine. Indeed, a temple was dedicated to the Holy Mother at the site by Swami Saradananda within only three years of her death.

A close scrutiny of the extant literature on Sarada, mostly in the form of personal reminiscences and anecdotes, suggests that the traffic between Jairambati and other places in Bengal, including East Bengal (pre-Partition; now Bangladesh) districts, substantially increased after 1910. This was a period by when the difficulties of travelling to Jairambati had also eased considerably. Jairambati and Kamarpukur, separated by only about five miles, were particularly infamous as places almost perennially affected by malarial fever. The area was virtually unapproachable in the rainy season due to the slushy terrain and widespread flooding. It was only in 1905 that the Bengal Nagpur Railway opened a line to Vishnupur, the local sub-divisional town. Prior to that date, the most frequented route to Jairambati passed through Bardhaman and the journey was made by a combination of travel by foot and bullock carts. Another route lay through Jehanabad, Arambagh and Tarakeswar. This was a shorter route but notorious as a dacoit-infested area. Bullock carts plying on this route preferred to travel together in large groups so as to escape being waylaid by dacoits. On the route lay large empty stretches of land, desolate and thinly populated and it was while crossing one of these lonely and deserted stretches, locally called 'Telo Bhelor Maath' (Telo Bhelo fields), that Sarada Devi accosted Sagar Santra, a fearsome Bagdi private bodyguard employed by the local zamindar who had also sporadically taken to robbery. We shall know more of that episode shortly, but there is little reason to doubt that road travel between the metropolis of Calcutta and the rural interior in Bengal was tiring, troublesome and hazardous. People preferred to travel by night so as to avoid the hot sun and fatigue, but that also exposed them to problems of a different kind such as locating suitable halting places. Most travellers to Jairambati could not afford the luxury of engaging bullock carts. Sarada Devi herself was often forced to travel on foot a good part of the way to save on expenses, particularly given the fact that she was often accompanied by an entourage comprising her nieces, devotees and other acquaintances. Understandably enough, procuring railway tickets for such a large party was well beyond her means. The occasional train ride or travelling by bullock carts for part of the way was made possible through contributions made by Ramakrishna monks, primarily Saradananda, who was the principal conduit through whom donations made by Western devotees reached Calcutta. The hazards and uncertainties of travel between Jairambati and either Dakshineswar or other places in Calcutta, where Saradamani was made to camp, casts some doubt on the view that people were easily tempted to visit these places by the promise of free meals and the initiating mantra. Sarada Devi, as we shall presently see, was a generous and caring host who treated her guests with genuine care, affection and exemplary hospitality. On the other hand, she was all too aware of certain operative constraints. Even at the height of her personal fame, she discouraged devotees from camping at Kamarpukur, Sri Ramakrishna's birthplace, for fear that they simply would not be fed adequately or well looked after. She herself visited Kamarpukur infrequently, never staying back for extended periods, which suggests a somewhat strained relationship between herself and her husband's larger family. Jairambati, which she inhabited more frequently, had its own problems. That she had to live here for extended periods forced her to respect local social conventions. Sarada Devi freely and uninhibitedly met the Western disciples of Vivekananda in the relatively less conservative environment of Calcutta, breaking all ritual taboos and restrictions; on the contrary, she discouraged Nivedita from visiting Jairambati. Surprisingly, another well-known figure connected with the Ramakrishna movement who somehow never visited either Jairambati or Kamarpukur was Swami Vivekananda himself. After 1886, when grinding poverty and the lack of adequate care forced Sarada Devi to spend more time at Calcutta under the care of monks of the Ramakrishna Order, approaching her would have been far from easy. Until the time she moved to the Udbodhan Press Office in Bagbazar in north Calcutta, she had no fixed place of residence and was made to frequently change her quarters. None of these had adequate space to host her devotees who had come to meet her after travelling long distances.

The Bride Marked with a Straw

In rural Bengal, it was a common custom among peasants and cultivators to set aside a particularly fine specimen of some fruit or vegetable first to be harvested in a season by wrapping a piece of straw around these. A fruit or vegetable so marked was treated as consecrated to God and was not to be sold at the market.

Around 1857–58, Sri Ramakrishna was in a state of intense spiritual ecstasy. By this time, he had moved from worshipping the Divine Mother, Kali, in iconic form to worshipping Her in the spirit. He never had cared much for formal scriptural knowledge and religious training came mostly in the form of oral instructions made by other holy men and women whom he had met in the course of his *sadhana* or spiritual praxis. But even as he evolved spiritually, a sense of mental uneasiness and bodily discomfort came to affect him increasingly. He turned restless and anxious, troubled by a burning sensation that began to physically affect his body and limbs. At the behest of his chief patron, Mathuranath

Biswas (d.1871), the best physicians from Calcutta were called in and yet, none could correctly diagnose his malady nor prescribe an effective remedy. At that stage, apparently, there was not enough reason to doubt that Ramakrishna was suffering not from some rare disease but a physiognomic condition produced by severe and highly unusual yogic practices. Sri Ramakrishna's pain and discomfort showed no signs of abating and it was naturally assumed that this was brought on by the aggravated and continuous pining to catch a vision of the Divine Mother, to be face to face with Her and to 'realize' Her luminous presence. Ramakrishna refused to believe that the image of the Goddess Kali that was routinely worshipped at Dakshineswar was no more than an insentient artifact that human hands had designed. He was desperate to reach behind the veil of illusion (*maya*) that the goddess was believed to have cast around her and which only the true *sadhaka* or spiritual practitioner could penetrate.

Soon, word about Ramakrishna's frenzied spiritual state reached his immediate family members at Kamarpukur and it worried them to hear that people in and around Dakshineswar were increasingly giving up on a man whose highly spiritual character could not be otherwise doubted. However, it now began to be widely rumoured that Gadadhar (as Sri Ramakrishna was commonly called by his family members) had somehow turned insane or was possessed by some particularly evil spirit who proved difficult to appease. Sri Ramakrishna's mother, Chandramani Devi, believed as every mother was perhaps apt to do, that good care and proper rest at home, freed from the routine duties carried out at the Dakshineswar temple would cure her son of his troubling ailment. By then, unfortunately, the eldest of her sons, Ramkumar, had passed away and hence, Chandramani Devi had to call upon her other surviving son, Rameswar, to arrange for Gadadhar's temporary return to Kamarpukur. By the end of the year 1858, the seemingly deranged man was back among his people with whom he was to spend over a year.

However, life at Kamarpukur did not prove to be very different from what it was in Dakshineswar. Notwithstanding the reassuring love and affection that he found under the care of his mother, Ramakrishna continued to spend most of his time at the local cremation ground, often late into the night, carrying out the most unusual and difficult of meditative practices. His close relatives found no comfort in the fact that he preferred to spend more time in self-imposed confinement at the most desolate of places than at home. The village elders and Chandramani Devi herself thus gradually came around to the view that perhaps the only effective remedy to Gadadhar's extraordinary condition was to implicate him in worldly ties. Marriage and the challenges of raising a family, they hoped, would prove to be a useful and effective distraction. Initially, what made them somewhat unsure or hesitant was the seeming improbability of Ramakrishna at all agreeing to a marriage at a time when his mind was preoccupied with very different things. They were also under some duress regarding the choice of a suitable bride. In the first place, the groom was already 23 years of age, well past the average age of marriage for upper-caste males. But more importantly, news of Ramakrishna's eccentric behaviour may have been common knowledge in Kamarpukur and its adjacent areas and probably dissuaded or discouraged some families that may have been otherwise interested in marital negotiations. It was Chandramani Devi's belief that a relatively older girl would better suit her son, but such a choice proved particularly difficult because of the high bride price demanded by the bride's family. It is hard to be definitive about just how this practice originated since it was far more common for the groom's party to make monetary demands in the form of dowries. Three possible explanations could be offered here. First, it could be that this arose in the relatively lower ritual rank that the Chattopadhyays were deemed to carry with respect to the Mukhopadhyays, a system that commonly worked among *kulin* or high ranking Brahmins in rural Bengal. This is not improbable, but unlikely. Second, it is possible that this followed from a demographic imbalance between the sexes in the region. If so, this had to be an extraordinary situation since in areas where *kulin* marriages were common, the number of high ranking men were usually fewer than women of an equivalent or lower class. Third, and this looks like the most cogent explanation, which could have been simply a matter of local custom.

Surprisingly, Sri Ramakrishna himself offered no resistance to the idea of marriage and when the family had all but given up hopes of procuring a suitable bride, he somewhat prophetically directed them to the daughter of Ramchandra Mukhopadhyay of village Jairambati. 'You will find my bride there,' he said, and then teasingly added, 'Providence has already marked her with a straw!' The search party that went across from

Kamarpukur to Jairambati was pleasantly surprised to find that the Mukhopadhyay family indeed had a marriageable girl, Saradamani, aged only five at the time. Five was a rather tender age for marriage for orthodox Hindu communities; even the most auspicious betrothal of a daughter was deemed to take place when she was eight (*gauridaan*). It is worth speculating, therefore, if the choice of Ramakrishna as the groom was in some way aided by his standing as a respectable, if also eccentric, priest and by the reputation that his father Khudiram Chattopadhyay had won in that region. Taken together, these may have outweighed any fears or anxiety that the Mukhopadhyay family might have had regarding the propriety of the match. The marriage was solemnized in May 1859 and even in this case, the groom's party could not escape paying a bride price of Rs 300, undoubtedly a substantial sum by contemporary standards. The marriage must have placed a heavy financial burden on Chandra Devi's family as can be inferred from the fact that the gold ornaments that the groom's party gifted to the new bride were in fact temporarily borrowed from an affluent neighbour, Dharmadas Laha, and not purchased on the occasion of the marriage, as was the convention. After the wedding ceremony was over and the time came for returning the ornaments, Chandramani was acutely embarrassed and did not have the heart to ask the child bride to part with them only a day after her wedding. The ornaments were actually taken off a sleeping Saradamani by Ramakrishna himself. The girl was heartbroken but Chandramani Devi somehow mollified her with the assurance that her husband would one day gift her better ornaments. This ruse so greatly offended an uncle of Sarada who had personally accompanied her on her first journey to Kamarpukur that he promptly carried his niece back to her parents in Jairambati.

Some contemporary scholars have argued that all her life, Sarada Devi herself carried a strong fascination for gold ornaments and cited some extraordinary reasons justifying her decision to continue wearing her gold bangles, even after being widowed, contrary to conventions. We shall have occasion to see why this view may not be as convincing as it prima facie appears to be. For now, it is enough to recall that Ramakrishna himself took a rather pragmatic view of this incident. Comforting his distraught mother, he argued how, regardless of the unhappiness or disappointment that the incident may have been caused in the community, the marriage itself could not be annulled! In any case, later he did buy his wife some gold ornaments from the money he was able to save, thanks to the munificence of his most generous patron, Mathuranath Biswas. He was also prudent enough to invest a part of the monthly stipend of Rs 7 that he received from the temple authorities at Dakshineswar with another great devotee and benefactor, Balaram Basu (1842–90), a wealthy man with considerable landholdings in Bengal and neighbouring Odisha. Basu also owned a retreat at Vrindavan, which was to later host Sarada Devi and her entourage. Our sources reveal that the money so invested yielded a return of Rs 60 annually, though apparently not for long. That apart, Sri Ramakrishna reportedly left cash savings of about Rs 400 for his wife. What happened of this money we do not quite know, but a possible explanation here is that it had to be spent on the upkeep of herself and her dependents. Following Ramakrishna's death in 1886, Saradamani stopped receiving the stipend of Rs 7 that she might have reasonably expected the Dakshineswar temple authorities to keep paying.

Somewhat against the wishes of his mother, Ramakrishna was back at Dakshineswar by the end of the year 1860. This could be ascribed to two reasons.

First, the pining to realize the Divine Mother, which had temporarily subsided in the affectionate care of Chandramani Devi, was back soon. After all, it was not the earthly mother that he was ultimately seeking but the Divine. Second, there was also the practical constraint of meeting household expenses for a family already affected by dwindling incomes. Sri Ramakrishna's only surviving brother, Rameswar, proved incapable of substantially augmenting the family income and it therefore occurred to Ramakrishna that the support of his Calcutta patrons might prove more valuable in arranging some financial relief to his family. It was probably for this reason that he also chose to bring along his aging mother to Dakshineswar to live with him. Chandramani Devi was to live on at Dakshineswar for some more years until her death in 1876.

As it turned out, the years following 1860 proved to be extremely valuable in the spiritual life of Ramakrishna. In the six years after 1860, he successively underwent training in Tantra under the female teacher, Bhairavi Yogeswari, in Vaishnava bhakti from a Ramait sadhu by the name of Jatadhari, in Advaita Vedanta under the Naga Sanyasi, Tota Puri, and in Sufi Islam under the supervision of the Hindu turned Sufi, Govinda Ray. In

1867, he was back in Kamarpukur in the company of his nephew, Hridayram Mukhpadhyay, and the Bhairavi Yogeswari. It was during this visit that he spent a sum of Rs 79 on purchasing scattered plots of land in the close vicinity of Kamarpukur: about one and a half bighas at Dompara and fourteen bighas at Sihor. To this must be added the small patrimony he inherited: a small stretch of fertile land that had once been gifted by one Sukhlal Goswami to his neighbour and friend, Khudiram Chattopadhyay. Compared to the recurring fracas that occurred between Sarada Devi's brothers over the distribution of family assets, male members of the Chattopadhyay family appear to have led more peaceful lives. One reason for this may simply have been the smaller number of male claimants. On the other hand, they were not quite charitable when it came to hosting Sarada herself or the swelling number of her devotees and casual visitors.

After the irate and offended uncle took her back to Jairambati, Saradamani could next set sight on her husband only in November 1860 when Ramakrishna himself called on his in-laws. She was then barely seven, but dutifully washed her husband's feet and fanned him, much to the merriment of her friends and relatives.

Reportedly, it was then that she visited Kamarpukur for the second time in the company of her husband. With Sri Ramakrishna back in Dakshineswar by the end of that year, her visits to Kamarpukur turned infrequent. Her third visit to her husband's family took place in April–May 1866 and lasted for about a month. She returned to Kamarpukur a fourth time during the winter of 1866–67 and this time, she stayed back for about six weeks. Both her husband and mother-in-law were, at the time, in Dakshineswar. The couple met soon thereafter when Ramakrishna visited Kamarpukur in the company of the Bhairavi Brahmani and Hriday Mukhopadhyay. This was one of his longest stays at his birthplace (for about seven months) and coincided with certain important developments. First, as we have earlier noted, Ramakrishna used some of his savings to invest in some land that was later registered as rent free *devotttar* (consecrated) property. More importantly, he used this occasion to tutor his wife in duties expected of a woman and wife in properly running a household, to behave appropriately with younger and older members of the extended family and to conduct herself with a detached dignity when dealing with neigbbours. In so doing, he played the role that ordinarily elderly women in the family, typically the mother-in-law, would play in relation to a newly-wedded bride. Sarada Devi may have benefited from the company of her mother-in-law only between 1872, when she first joined her husband at Dakshineswar, and 1876, when Chandramani Devi passed away. However, Ramakrishna is also known to have tutored his child bride in spiritual matters. This is an issue to which the hagiographers have paid a disproportionately great attention if only to rationalize both the spiritual potentiality unfolding in Sarada Devi and the good fortune of being tutored by the Master himself. Prima facie, it does seem somewhat unlikely that a seven-year-old girl even superficially understood the spiritual content of Sri Ramakrishna's discourse. On the other hand, she is quite likely to have retained some of the more captivating ideas that her husband articulated in the form of commonplace parables and preaching, for the man was a gifted storyteller with excellent communication skills. And he mostly used a rustic idiom and analogies drawn from the rhythms of everyday life in the Bengal countryside, with which his wife would have been all too familiar. In her adult life, Saradamani would never hesitate to express her indebtedness to the spiritual training imparted by her husband. Many of her own views on social or spiritual matters simply echo and amplify those of her husband; her own disciples have testified to the fact that Ramakrishna was always a living presence in her life both in thought and deed. In spiritual matters, she rarely spoke in the first person, always preferring to remind devotees about what Ramakrishna had himself said about a certain matter. On spiritual matters, she always took a backseat in relation to her husband.

Saradamani joined her husband at Dakshineswar in the spring of 1872. She was then a little short of twenty and beginning to develop a mature woman's instincts, habits and interests. It was indeed unusual of a newly-wedded wife to be separated from her husband for as long as fifteen years. Since 1859, when she was married, Sarada had caught sight of Ramakrishna only intermittently and never given the opportunity of leading a settled family. With advancing age, there had also awakened in her a greater self-consciousness as a woman and wife. At her age, it was only natural for a woman to want to be united with her husband in both body and mind. But that apart, she would also have been under some pressure from friends and relatives in Jairambati who expressed concern at the unusual life that Ramakrishna was reportedly leading at Dakshineswar. Her mother, Shyamasundari, and other village women naturally worried at the ways of the *pagla jamai* (the mad son-in-law). In all probability, some of them felt sorry for Saradamani for being so abandoned and having to put up with an abnormal conjugal life. Village gossip only added to Shyamasundari Devi's woes. Later, reflecting on the life of the Holy Mother, even Sister Nivedita came to believe that following the marriage, Ramakrishna had all but 'forgotten' his wife. At twenty, an average village woman of Bengal would have well entered motherhood, but which in this case, looked quite elusive. News of Ramakrishna's continued spiritual insomnia kept travelling to Jairambati and Kamarpukur. It was rumoured that the man often wept uncontrollably, wrung his hands in desperation and performed all kinds of unnatural acts. In common perception, he was in the middle of yet another spiritual crisis whereby the whirlwind of ecstatic feeling threatened to blow him away, leaving the man with the feeling of being mentally and physically shipwrecked. Understandably enough, Sarada worried for her husband and the duties of a wife personally taking charge of the situation soon seized her with some force. In early 1872, an opportunity came by rather unexpectedly. Coinciding with the birthday celebrations of the Vaishnava saint, Chaitanya (1486–1533), some women of Jairambati planned to travel to Calcutta to take a dip in the holy Ganges, as was customary. Saradamani confided in her father that she wished to join the party too. Ramchandra, reportedly, had the astuteness to realize that his daughter's true intentions were quite removed from what she outwardly expressed. Nearly five years had passed since the couple had last met and this did not augur well for them. Hence, he took it upon himself to personally escort his daughter all the way to Dakshineswar, where his son-in-law resided. They reached their destination late in the evening of an indeterminable day of March 1872, travelling mostly by foot. This and subsequent journeys that Saradamani made from Jairambati to Dakshineswar were eventful for one reason or the other and became the subject of much hagiographic speculation. On her first outing, Sarada, not quite used to such long journeys on foot, developed high fever en route. Legend has it that one night, when the travellers were resting, she found a comely girl of dark complexion comforting her in ways that eased her pain and discomfort. When quizzed, she said that she had come from Dakshineswar and assured Saradamani that her father and she would indeed reach their destination soon. It is only natural that those who piously believe this story, originating no doubt in Sarada Devi herself, also take the unknown girl to be Goddess Kali herself who interceded to guard Sarada against any misfortune and to ensure that she joined her husband who was himself a pious devotee of Kali. Such beliefs also connect rather well with what was to follow: Sarada's ably serving Sri Ramakrishna in her capacity as a devoted wife, consciously imbibing his essential teachings as a disciple and her progressively evolving into a cultic figure herself.

Contrary to what is expressed in certain quarters[1], Sri Ramakrishna was positively happy at Sarada's travelling all the way from Jairambati to be with him at Dakshinewar. His spontaneous feelings though were also that she had arrived a trifle too late since the 'good days' at Dakshineswar were seemingly coming to an

1 Narasingha P. Sil states that Ramakrishna was positively alarmed at Sarada's unexpected arrival at Dakhineswar since this was likely to tempt him back to the life of an ordinary householder and enter conjugal life which he was keen to avoid at all costs. Even allowing for hagiographic excesses, it has to be said that no biographer of Sarada has made claims to this effect.

end with the demise of Mathuranath the previous year. 'Oh, you come at a time when "Sejobabu" (the name commonly used for Mathuranath) is no more around to take good care of you,' he had wistfully confessed before his wife. In hindsight, it has to be said that Sarada's joining her husband at Dakshineswar proved to be opportune. Hriday Mukhopadhyay, Ramakrishna's nephew, who lived with him at Dakshineswar, was a faithful—if also a somewhat self-seeking—companion who aspired some of the spiritual prowess and fame that was being attached to his uncle. Also, Ramakrishna, by this time, had developed certain chronic ailments of his own, mostly from his poor digestive powers. The food cooked at the common kitchen at Dakshineswar did not suit him and made him suffer continuously from bouts of dysentery. The services of a wife who would properly attend to his special dietary needs proved greatly helpful and Ramakrishna counted on Saradamani to nurse him back to health. For about eight months or so, the couple lived together in the quarters assigned to Sri Ramakrishna himself. During this time, she mostly had to keep awake through the nights or suffer from interrupted sleep on account of the Master himself frequently entering a state of *samadhi*, whereby he turned inert and lost all bodily consciousness. This was a sight quite unfamiliar to the wife who felt helpless at not being able to prevent this or even bring back the husband to normal ways. Sarada Devi later narrated before her devotees that getting wind of her plight and predicament, Sri Ramakrishna taught her some methods by which she could assist in returning her husband to a normal state. As is now well known, the marriage went unconsummated for the entire length of time that Ramakrishna and his wife shared a common bed. It is also commonly believed that Ramakrishna openly asked Sarada if she intended to drag him back from a state of divine consciousness to one that was 'samsaric' or mundane and marked by base animal passion. 'People might even suggest that you secretly administer some drugs to get me back to the ways of a common man'—he once warned his wife— 'and please make sure that you do not give in to such nefarious designs.' Sarada Devi ultimately moved to the adjacent *nahabatkhana* (literally, the music chamber) when it became clear to even Ramakrishna that she would go sleepless in his ecstatic company.

It is not at all fortuitous that Dakshineswar also proved to be the site where Ramakrishna divinized (in the opinion of some critics, dehumanized) the human figure of Sarada, ritually worshipping her as a representation of the goddess Shodashi (literally, sixteen years of age)[2], with important and far-reaching consequences. It is highly unlikely too that he would have been able to carry this out in the rural setting of either Kamarpukur or Jairambati. In hindsight, it looks as though the exact date and site of the Shodashi Puja remained hidden from public knowledge for quite some time, leading to conflicting claims being made. Whereas the puja was held on 5 June 1872, Swami Saradananda's *Sri Sri Ramakrishna Lilaprasanga* places it exactly a year later.[3] Sarada herself summarily dismissed claims made by Ramchandra Dutta (1851–99), an influential householder devotee of Ramakrishna, that the puja was performed in Jairambati. It was simply impossible that her community would allow a man to so reverentially worship a woman and wife, she had jocularly pointed out.

2 Age was of no concern here, since at the time Sarada herself was close to nineteen. Hence, it was not as though Ramakrishna worshipped Sarada as the Shodashi, but the goddess residing in her.

3 The confusion of dates occurred primarily due to the fact that the special worship of Kali (Phahlaharini Kali Puja) fell on the same date in successive years.

Shodashi, also called Tripura Sundari and Lalita, is the object of adoration in the well known Sakta-Tantric classic, *Lalita Sahasranama* (A Thousand Verses in Praise of Lalita). She is taken to be one of the Dasamahavidyas (ten primeval female powers), who grants the devotee the highest state of spiritual consciousness. Sakti worship in this form essentially aimed at acquiring personal spiritual and ritual power and reportedly, Ramakrishna obtained his cue from Pundit Gaurikanta Tarkabagish (called Gauri Pundit in the *Sri Sri Ramakarishna Kathamrita*), a visitor who called upon Ramakrishna at Dakshineswar. Gauri Pundit had similarly worshipped his wife as Shodashi, an event far less known or celebrated in the relevant literature. In the case of Ramakrishna, however, this was seen to carry multiple meanings, at least as far as his official biographers are concerned. Such biographers are agreed upon the view that this led to the sublimation of human carnal desire into a higher state of consciousness. Worshipping the woman or wife was tantamount to locating in her the manifestations of the Divine Mother. Arguably, this desexualized the woman, transforming her from an object of male desire to benign Motherhood. On another level, this also rescued the son from committing incestuous love. Our sources suggest that the Shodashi Puja was carried out late at night, well hidden from public view. The ceremony included Sri Ramakrishna first changing Sarada's garments, followed by acts of ritually worshipping and feeding the goddess. Upon being later probed, Sarada Devi confessed to have had no bodily consciousness of what transpired for the entire length of the ceremony. One of the close relatives to cast some doubt upon this testimony was Ramakrishna's niece, Laxmimani Ghatak, who simply would not understand just how her aunt would have no memory whatsoever of what she underwent.

For Ramakrishna, if some contemporary critics are to be believed, the Shodashi Puja was essentially a way of ensuring that his wife would henceforth make no sexual demands on her husband, thereby protecting his continence and *sadhana*. The question to ask here is if such de-sexualizing of the wife and inhibiting her natural sexual urges was traditionally accepted as an integral part of the ritual process. There is no information in the *Kathamrita* or other related sources to suggest that Gauri Pundit, who inspired Ramakrishna, himself abstained from cohabitation with his wife following the Shodashi Puja. There is also a deeper conflict that we might address here, however briefly. Both marriage and raising a progeny were part of established rites *(sanskaras)* for upper-caste males and it does seem somewhat odd that Sri Ramakrishna agreed to follow one and not the other. When he chose to marry Sarada, could he have counted upon her agreeing to lead a life of sexual self-denial? In hindsight, this exception makes sense only from a hagiographical perspective, which might suggest that Sri Ramakrishna had some means of knowing that his wife would readily give in to his wishes only because she was destined to be his spiritual partner and not a sexually potent wife. Saradamani herself is reported to have said how those who alleged cruelty and unnatural treatment on the part of her husband, committed the grave error of taking the woman to be an object of physical gratification alone. Prima facie, this seems much too close to the monastic view on man-woman relationships to be entirely her free judgment.

From a close scrutiny of the available sources, it is possible to recount the sequence of Saradamani's travels between Jairambati and Dakshineswar in Ramakrishna's lifetime. However, the chronology provided in various sources is often uncertain and conflicting. Also, while we may be reasonably sure about the time the outward journey from Jairambati began, the same cannot be said about the journey back. There were at least eight such visits in all, between March 1872 and March 1885 as listed below:

First visit: commenced in March 1872; returned in October 1873.

Second visit: commenced April 1874, returned September 1875.

Third visit: commenced 17 March 1876, returned November 1876.

Fourth visit: commenced February 1878, returned early 1879.

Fifth visit: commenced February–March 1881.

Sixth visit: commenced February–March 1882.

Seventh visit: commenced March 1884.

Eighth visit: commenced March 1885.

Of the 13 years separating 1872 (her first trip to Dakshineswar) and 1885 (her last), about ten were spent in the company of Ramakrishna.[4]

From the above list, it is clear that allowing for some exceptions, Sarada Devi visited her husband

4 I have largely followed the chronology provided by Narasingha P. Sil. This chronology does not always tally with that prepared by Renuka Chattopadhyay and included in Swami Purnatmananda's edited *Yugajanani Sarada* (3rd ed. 2001; pp. 497–511). Going by Chattopadhyay's version, there were only seven visits. In this version, the fourth visit occurred in 1881, leaving an unusually long gap between the third visit in 1876 and the fourth that reportedly took place in 1881.

at Dakshineswar once every year on an average. It is not clear though why her stay at Dakshineswar never exceeded a year at a time. In certain cases, apparently, she was forced to leave promptly, as for instance, in 1881 when Hriday humiliated Shyamasundari Devi and her daughter on their arrival in Dakshineswar, or else in 1884 when Ramakrishna himself asked her to return to Jairambati and prepare for yet another visit allegedly because she had begun her original journey on an inauspicious day. He also took this as the reason for his having dislocated a bone on his left hand. Yet another time (February–March 1881) she was especially summoned to Dakshineswar by Ramakrishna himself who complained that his newly recruited nephew, Ramlal, who had replaced the disgraced Hriday,[5] was not taking good care of him. On her last visit to Dakshineswar, Saradamani had to move house as Ramakrishna himself was shifted to Calcutta for medical treatment. Thereafter, she kept following her husband as

5 Hriday tried to emulate the ways of his illustrious uncle by ritually worshipping the young daughter of Trailokyanath Biswas, Mathuranath's successor as the proprietor of the Dakshineswar temple premises. This greatly displeased the father who feared that a Brahmin's worshipping a non-Brahmin was highly inauspicious and would bring him misfortune. Hriday was summarily dismissed from service for this act of transgression.

he was moved from one rented house to another until his death in August 1886.

It is not entirely unlikely that Sarada herself found it difficult to stay on at Dakshineswar for long stretches given the practical difficulties she faced in everyday life. Persistent illness affected her health, both at Dakshineswar and Jairambati. At Dakshineswar, she was continually stricken by acute dysentery and the dampness in the air which greatly emaciated her and forced her to go back to her village from time to time. Persistent and acute dysentery, it may be recalled, had driven her to seek the intercession of Goddess Singhabahini, one who is believed to have therapeutic powers. In Jairambati itself, heavily infested as it was with mosquitoes, she developed an enlarged spleen for which again she sought local cure at the neighbouring village of Kayapat. It is equally possible that being born and bred in the open countryside, she found life in Calcutta quite stifling and constricted. Such differences persisted for the rest of her life. At a time when she began to be widely respected by monks and laymen alike, living in Calcutta certainly offered more material comforts. For one, when in Calcutta, she did not have to devote much time and energy to growing and gathering her food, which she was compelled to do for a time when living in Kamarpukur and at Jairambati. In her own village, she had to put up with all kinds of petty rivalries, jealousy and social opposition for the kind of life she led or the social digressions she sometimes performed. Not adhering to established conventions was challenging; on one occasion, she had to face near rebellion from local Brahmins who refused to accept food served by novices of the Ramakrishna Order on the ground that their caste identity was undisclosed or unknown. The matter was settled only after she agreed to pay a punitive fine.

Another eventful journey especially highlighted by hagiographers is Sarada Devi's encounter with a dacoit en route from Kamarpukur to Calcutta. This event probably dates back to the year 1876 (coinciding with her third visit to Dakshineswar), though in the absence of reliable sources, we cannot be absolutely sure. That year too, Sarada Devi decided to accompany a party of men and women travelling from Kamarpukur to Calcutta for a ritual bath in the Ganges. We do also know that in this instance, she was accompanied by Laxmimani Ghatak and Shibram, the daughter and son of Ramakrishna's elder brother, Rameswar. Somewhere between Arambagh and Tarakeswar lay the dreaded and desolate Telo Bhelo fields and the travellers were anxious that this stretch be covered before nightfall so as to avoid being waylaid by dacoits. However, the party comprised of some old women who proved unable to walk more briskly. The rest of the party, concerned about their own safety, hurried towards Tarakeswar, leaving Sarada and the other women behind. Rather than desert her old companions on the way, Sarada Devi preferred to walk along with them even though this slackened her own pace. Predictably, by the time they were midway through the Telo Bhelo fields, it had turned pitch dark. Much to their horror, the women soon found a fearsome figure, by all appearances—a dacoit, approaching them rapidly. The man rudely inquired where the women were heading. Reportedly, Sarada did not lose her presence of mind and in a gentle, endearing voice, she introduced herself as the man's young daughter who was travelling to join her husband at Dakshineswar. By all available accounts, the innocence and the trusting tone in which this was said brought about a change in the man. The man was in the company of his wife and together, the couple escorted Sarada to the local village, after which they arranged for some refreshment and a good night's sleep. Next morning, Sarada rejoined the rest of the party.

The man who appeared to be a fearsome dacoit has now been identified as one Sagar Santra, a Bagdi henchman who served the *pattanidar*s (lessees) of the local village by the name of Telo. Dacoity and brigandage may not have been his major occupation for the man was also an amateur actor often enlisted in folk theatrical performances called *Krishnayatra.* He is believed to have died from a fall sometime in 1910–11. Interestingly enough, Saradamani's encounter with the man taken to be a dacoit (Dakat Baba or the dacoit father as he is now called) proved to be valuable hagiographic material in the hands of devotees. It was a story she herself enjoyed narrating before some of her Western disciples. By common belief, Sagar Santra had a vision of Goddess Kali, whom dacoits in Bengal both feared and revered as a rule, in the course of his meeting Sarada Devi. He is also known to have subsequently called on Sarada and Ramakrishna at Dakshineswar. Most importantly, he is believed to have been the first man before whom Sarada revealed her 'true identity'. The other person who fully believed in the veracity of the story was Shibram, Ramakrishna's nephew. We have no means of confirming if Shibram was a witness to what occurred at Telo Bhelo; on the other hand, as a person who had accompanied Sarada on this trip, he naturally attached great importance to Sarada's testimony, which is about the only direct source of information available on this episode. Once en route to Jairambati, Shibram accosted Saradamani with the demand that she reaffirm her identity with Goddess Kali. Regardless of whether or not this story is credible, what ought to interest us is the growing public interest attached to it. In 1965, there came into existence Telua Sarada Ramakrishna Sevashram, an organization clearly founded and supported by enthusiastic disciples and devotees of Sarada Devi. About a decade later (in 1977), a temple was constructed at the site where the young Saradamani fearlessly confronted the threat from a menacing dacoit and disarmingly won him over.[6]

A Sita in Exile

In adult life, and especially after she acquired a good number of devotees and disciples, Saradamani would at times identify herself with Radha and Sita, two well known figures drawn from Hindu mythology

6 A full-length monograph describing this episode was published in 1994 by Tadit Kumar Bandopadhyay called *Sri Sri Ma O Dakat Baba*.

and around which religious cults have been known to grow up. However, it was the connecting thread between the three that is of greater interest here. Both Radha and Sita are known to have suffered pangs of separation (*viraha*) and neglect from their lovers or married partners as the case may be. They were also known to lead lonesome lives and called upon to make recurring sacrifices to appease orthodox society. In the case of Sarada Devi, apart from being a matter of self-description, the comparison drawn between say, Sita and Saradamani was reinforced by comments made by visitors to Dakshineswar who called on Sarada at the *nahabatkhana*), a two-storied structure that was located in close vicinity of Ramakrishna's own quarters.

The *nahabatkhana* was the place that Sarada Devi made her home after spending a few months in the room occupied by Ramakrishna. It was also a particularly uncomfortable place to be living in. It was cramped, ill lit and without adequate ventilation. On the other hand, the comfort of living in more spacious quarters may not have been the most important consideration for Saradamani. In 1876, another influential patron of Ramakrishna, Sambhunath Mallik, had a small cottage built for her in close vicinity. Sarada abandoned this place and shifted back to the *nahabat* once her husband himself began to suffer from acute dysentery and required constant care.

The ground floor of the *nahabat* measured about 50 square feet with octagonal walls, each measuring about 3 feet each and with a ceiling that measured less than 9 feet high. It was surrounded on all sides by a bamboo screen ensuring privacy, but allowing little air to pass through. The room was stocked with all kinds of groceries with even live fish in earthen pots hanging from the ceiling. It was the residence for two kinds of people: people who lived with Sarada permanently or else for long stretches of time and other visitors and close companions who were put up for a night or two. To the former category belonged Laxmimani, Ramakrishna's widowed niece who stayed on the premises between 1872 and 1885. She was a companion that Sarada Devi always had, and even Ramakrishna had the good humour to call the two 'a pair of caged birds'! Others who stayed on the premises for fairly long spells of time were some of Ramakrishna's close female devotees: Gopaler Ma (Aghoremani Devi, 1822–1906), a widow and strict vegetarian whose special wooden stove had to be doused with holy water from the Ganges every time she cooked, Gauri Ma (Mridani

Chattopadhyay, 1857–1938), Golap Ma (Golapsundari Devi, d. 1924), Yogin Ma (Yogindramohini Biswas, 1851–1924) and Nikunja Devi, wife of the Ramakrishna diarist, Mahendranath Gupta (1854–1932). Chandramani Devi, Sri Ramakrishna's mother, lived on the upper floor which was also used for hosting women visitors from Calcutta who opted to stay back for a night. The corpulent, well dressed Calcutta women never dared to enter Sarada's room, which had a particularly low door, with the result that unsuspecting visitors often banged their heads against it. They chose to stand at the door, holding on to the door jamb and commented on the 'pitiable' conditions that the permanent boarders had to undergo. Initially, Sarada herself suffered quite a few blows to her head when entering her room, though later, as she was to wittily observe, her head would by itself bow down as she prepared to enter her room! The *nahabatkhana* had no toilet attached to it, and there was none even in close vicinity. This forced Sarada and her companions to leave bed by dawn and go down to the river. Once, in the faint light at the break of dawn, she unwittingly stepped on a crocodile which had climbed on to the mud banks. Thereafter, she would carry a lamp whenever walking that path. It was deeply embarrassing for women to go down to the river for sanitary purposes in broad daylight, with the result that they were forced to desist from visiting the latrine for long hours at a stretch. It was Sarada's feeling that this unnatural regime itself caused some of her recurring ailments. A small latrine was built close to the *nahabatkhana* only as late as 1884 at the behest of Yogin Ma.

So silent and stealthy were Sarada's movements in and out of the *nahabatkhana* that employees of the Dakshineswar temple complex were heard saying that while they had heard of Sarada living on the same premises they had never actually seen her. Ramakrishna was keen that his wife led a disciplined life, and often forced Sarada and Laxmimani to leave bed at dawn by pouring cold water on their mattresses. Sarada's own duties consisted primarily of cooking for her husband and personally carrying the food to him every afternoon and evening. Meal times were the only occasions when she would meet her husband in the course of a day. For a long time, she kept herself veiled even in the presence of her husband and discontinued this practice only after a female devotee from Kashi persuaded her to do so. After the passing away of Ramakrishna in 1886, she went back to her old routines, never unveiling herself before an adult male who was not a close relative. While at the *nahabatkhana*, the only two men that she directly spoke to were Gopal Senior (Gopal Ghosh, Swami Advaitananda, 1828–1909) and Latu (Rakhtu Ram, Swami Adbhutananda, d.1920). There is reason to believe that even Vivekananda may not have caught sight of the Holy Mother's face. The Swami also took care not to touch her feet but paid his respects from a distance. Many other disciples were not as reasonable or understanding and they often forced Sarada Devi to endure the extremely exhausting ordeal of remaining wrapped in a cloth from head to foot even on a hot summer day in Calcutta. Some were even known to gently bite her so that the pain might serve to remind her of them even later!

It would seem that Sarada was allowed to briefly venture out of the *nahabat* at times when the temple complex was completely deserted. For instance, she made rounds of Brahmin families residing in the close vicinity of the temple. One such family was that of the Pandeys who especially invited her home on festive occasions. She always left using a less-frequented pathway, slipping out inconspicuously through a small side gate and so timed her return to the temple premises that no one would notice her movements. Her return journey to the *nahabat* usually occurred when visitors and local villagers were busy watching the evening *arati,* the ritual worship of Goddess Kali.

The *nahabat* functioned as some sort of a free kitchen, though catering largely to devotees in the Ramakrishna circle. Judging by the quantity of food cooked each day and the number of people fed, it has to be said that this would not have been possible without financial assistance coming from generous patrons. We do know that the philanthropist Suresh Mitra paid a sum of Rs 10 every month and it is quite likely that some help also came intermittently from other supporters of the movement, as for instance, Mahendranath Gupta and possibly Ramchandra Dutta as well. Reportedly, about 3.5 seers (approximately 2.8 kilograms) of wheat flour were required each day for preparing leaven breads (rotis). By one estimate, the number required ranged between 150 and 200 rotis every day. From this it is possible to deduce a few things. First, that a good number of visitors who could lay claim to a free meal cooked at the *nahabat* turned up every day at Dakshineswar, and second, that cooking on such a large scale could not have been possible without some help coming from extra hands. Sri Ramakrishna himself instructed Latu to help Sarada by kneading the dough and carry out other sundry duties. The daily shopping was carried out by another direct disciple of Ramakrishna, Gopal Senior, and presumably, younger ladies in Sarada Devi's entourage, as for instance, Laxmimani assisted her with cooking. That Bengali bhadraloks had developed a taste for coarse rotis and spicy lentils in preference to a meal of rice and fish does come as a surprise but this is precisely what devotees like Ramchandra Dutta and his better-known cousin, Narendranath Dutta (Swami Vivekananda), often demanded upon their arrival at Dakshineswar. Once, when Ramakrishna asked Narendranath, whether he had enjoyed the meal at the *nahabat*, the latter grudgingly reported that he felt rather sickly upon eating it. Discreet inquiries revealed that the food cooked that day had been a bland meal routinely partaken by Bengalis, in Ramakrishna's own words, a meal not spicy enough to make a hog grunt! After 1879, by when he had begun nominally initiating some young men into a life of renunciation, Sri Ramakrishna kept close watch over just how the *nahabat* kitchen was handling his trusted devotees. He suspected that Sarada Devi, out of motherly affection, was overfeeding the boys and hence, he took it upon himself to fix their quota of rotis: Rakhal (Rakhalchandra Ghosh, Swami Brahmananda, 1863–1922) was allowed six, Latu five, Gopal Senior and Baburam (Baburam Ghosh, Swami Premananda, 1861–1918) only four each. Men who aspired to be monks had to cultivate a sense of self-discipline and restraint, the Master maintained. In the late 1870s, by when Ramakrishna's fame as an extraordinary spiritual figure began to spread in colonial Calcutta, the presence of a good number of devotees at Dakshineswar assumed some social and strategic importance. It was important that even when pursuing a spiritual life, monks and devotees also felt contented and well cared for in their everyday lives. At the end of their meals, guests were sometimes served with betel leaves (paan) laced with the choicest condiments. 'Bhaktas (devotees) had to be looked after well for and gradually won over,' Sarada Devi was heard to have said.

There is a certain twist to the tale of Sarada's life at Dakshineswar, which would be interesting to include. It appears as though the ordinary employees at the temple did not take kindly to Sarada's joining her husband and beginning to live within the premises. They noticed that after a time, devotees calling on Sri Ramakrishna also began to pay respects to his wife by way of offering small gifts of food or other items. Envious of such practices, they spread the word that Thakur (Ramakrishna) had conspired to have his wife live with him, so as to augment his personal income. Ramakrishna's own reactions to this allegation are not known, but it is quite likely that Sarada herself got wind of this and would have been the source of this information for later biographers. Lower-rung employees of the temple appear to have disliked the couple and looked for small pretexts to embarrass them. Within a few months of Ramakrishna's death, they conspired to have his stipend discontinued, placing Sarada Devi in serious financial trouble. As an aside, it might also be mentioned that Saradamani herself nursed some unhappiness about Ramakrishna's vocation. It was tragic that a man born of such a pious and ritually upright family as the Chattopadhyays of Kamarpukur was compelled to serve an establishment built by a woman from the lowly Kaibarta caste, she once remarked.

Life after Ramakrishna

In April 1885, Sri Ramakrishna was diagnosed with 'clergyman's throat', an older name for throat cancer.

On 26 September that year, he was moved to the residence of a wealthy householder devotee, Balaram Basu (1842–90), in north Calcutta. To enable medical practitioners attending on him visit more frequently, he was subsequently (2 October) moved to a rented house in Shyampukur. Sarada Devi joined him a few days later, travelling from Dakshineswar. Here Ramakrishna remained for about two weeks until the place was found cramped for space and uncongenial. The devotees next rented (11 December 1885) a sprawling estate at Kashipur with lush greenery. Here there was no dearth of space and Sarada Devi could be given a room all to herself. However, Kashipur Udyan (Kashipur Garden House) posed a new kind of problem. For one, it was at a considerable distance from north or central Calcutta where most intimate devotees and disciples of Ramakrishna ordinarily resided. Daily commuting proved difficult and expensive with the result that a kitchen serving the needs of about half a dozen people had to be started at Kashipur itself. This naturally added to the expenses. The monthly rent to the premises was about Rs 80 and was paid entirely by Suresh Mitra. Balaram Basu paid for Ramakrishna's special diet and Ramchandra Dutta for the regular meals served to others.

When Ramakrishna's disease showed no signs of abatement, Sarada Devi decided to visit the well-known Siva shrine at Tarakeswar, so that she might pray for some relief to her ailing husband. She spent about three days at the site without the benefit of any divine vision or prophecy, as was usually expected to occur in such instances. On the contrary, one night, she suddenly and quite unexpectedly woke up to a loud noise and felt gripped by an intense feeling about the very impermanence of the world and of everything that was a part of it. Who was the husband and who the wife, an unknown voice inside her appeared to cry out! She returned to Kashipur, dejected, but also better reconciled to her fate.

Predictably, even the best of human concern and care failed to avert the inevitable and Sri Ramakrishna breathed his last a little past midnight on 16 August 1886. Reportedly, only a cry of deep anguish escaped Sarada's lips: 'O Mother Kali,' she cried out, 'for what fault of mine have you forsaken me!' Prima facie, it is perplexing that Sarada should identify her husband with the Goddess, for she is otherwise known to have endorsed the idea expressed by Sri Ramakrishna himself that the two of them were but intimate female companions (*sakhis*) to the Goddess. In later life, when she had been widely accepted in her status as the ubiquitous mother, she also added further complexity to the matter by suggesting that she also looked upon her husband as her son!

Biographical literature on Saradamani reports that Ramakrishna trusted his wife to continue his spiritual mission. 'The people of Calcutta were sunk in worldliness, only wriggling around like lowly worms,' he had told Sarada a few days before passing away, 'See to it that they are rescued.' That apart, as was typical of the man, Sri Ramakrishna also gave his wife some practical advice, evidently with an air of concern:

> 'Never give up your association with Kamarpukur,' he warned her, 'if need be grow some greens to go with your daily meal of rice but never seek monetary help form anybody or seek somebody's shelter. I bless so that you may never be found wanting in a modest meal and a coarse cloth to wrap around your body.'

In hindsight, we know that Sarada did struggle, albeit only in vain, to secure for herself a place at Kamarpukur. Allegedly, Ramakrishna's nephews mistreated her and denied her a rightful share in the property. Immediately following her husband's death, she had to pass through a particularly bad patch when on days she could not afford to buy herself even some salt for her meals. Other than Saradamani herself, the person who felt most pained and humiliated by this turn of events was Shyamasundari herself, who repeatedly invited her daughter to move to Jairambati but to no avail. The daughter proved stubbornly self-respectful and for a time, resisted all attempts at relocating herself. It is reasonable to assume that in this her decision was guided by the poverty that her mother herself faced. At some point, however, she was forced to yield to her mother's wishes. Mahendranath Gupta, generally noted for his accuracy with facts, tells us that hereafter, Sarada lived in Kamarpukur only for brief periods: in October 1890, July to October of 1891, July 1892, the months of January and July of 1893, May 1895 to January 1896 and between May and October 1897. Apparently, this list excludes the shorter visits she occasionally made to Jairambati, as for instance, on the occasion of the annual Jagaddhatri Puja held in November, first instituted by Shyamasundari Devi in 1877.

There is a popular belief to the effect that as Sarada Devi was preparing to cast off signs of a married Hindu woman, as for instance, the gold bangles she wore on her wrists and the vermilion mark traditionally worn on the forehead, Sri Ramakrishna appeared in a vision and forbade her to carry this out. He denied that he had at all passed on to a different life, which then permitted Sarada not to adopt the attire usually worn by high-caste Hindu Bengali widows. Reportedly, Ramakrishna further vindicated this aberrant behaviour by suggesting that Sarada consult her friend and companion, Gauri Ma, on this matter. Here, his reference was to Vaishnava shastras, which maintained all women had Lord Krishna as their immortal husband and hence, the demise of the earthly husband did not necessarily transform them to the state of widowhood.[7] Having so consulted Gauri Ma on her first tour of Vrindavan in 1886, Sarada Devi chose to wear a single gold bangle on her wrists and saris with a thin red border, both of which would have been ordinarily

7 This is an idea commonly associated with the Rajput queen, Mirabai, who composed songs celebrating Lord Krishna as her wedded husband even with her earthly husband alive. In some parts of India, devadasis or dancing girls attached to temples were ritually wedded to the presiding deity; hence the name devadasi or servitor to the Lord.

forbidden to a Brahmin widow. Unlike Laxmimani, she did not also have her hair shaved. Her diet, however, remained within conventional bounds, sans fish or flesh though to the best of our knowledge, she may not have scrupulously observed ritual vows and fasts that a widow was obliged to do every month. Photographs of her now propagated and widely distributed through the digital media by the Ramakrishna Order show her as wearing a fairly conspicuous vermillion mark on her forehead that is ordinarily restricted to women with living husbands only.[8] This stands in some contrast to photographs of her taken at Jairambati and other places in rural Bengal where she can be seen draped simply in a plain white borderless sari. Apparently, Sarada Devi was careful not to offend the socially more conservative villagers.

Choices of this kind and their social approval are perhaps best understood as matters of pious belief. Surely, the daily life of upper-caste Hindu widows has undergone significant changes since the late 19th

8 This is quite obvious from the official collection of photographs first published in 1990 by the Udbodhan Press. The eighth reprint (2019) of this collection, a copy of which I have, carries on its front jacket a photograph of the marble bust of Sarada Devi adorning an ornate, red bordered sari and conspicuous vermillion marks on her forehead.

century. Though still preferring sobriety in sartorial matters, upper-caste Hindu widows no longer have their heads shaved or to go without food and drink on designated days of the month. Even Brahmin widows are now known to consume non-vegetarian food and participate in family festivities, albeit with a sense of disinterested detachment. On the other hand, for a widow to adorn signs that only a woman with a living husband may adopt (as for instance, a red bordered sari, the vermilion mark and the conspicuous presence of gold ornaments) would still be rare even among educated, urban widows whose attachment to the traditional religious and ritual life of Hindus was otherwise at best tenuous. The situation in Saradamani's own time, one imagines, would have been decidedly different. And yet her choices appear to have avoided lasting social controversy. We do hear of objections raised by some women devotees such as the wife of Manomohan Mitra, a devotee of Sri Ramakrishna, who found Sarada's retaining the gold ornament quite unbecoming of a respectable Brahmin widow. We must also allow for the fact that Sarada Devi was otherwise taken to be an ideal Hindu widow: chaste, pious, selfless, unassuming and strongly loyal to the memory of her husband. Also, she never hesitated to admit that both her spiritual life and the social had been strongly shaped by her husband's presence. The more intriguing part is not so much Sarada Devi making extraordinary choices, but their increasing social acceptance. The question to ask here is whether Sarada's pronounced departures from social conventions were employed both by herself and her followers to further canonize religious charisma.

Contemporary scholars have cast doubt over Sarada's citing Ramakrishna's authority, interpreting the episode as a manipulative ploy that she used to sanctify her alleged fondness and fascination for gold ornaments. There is really no way of telling just where the truth lies. Such a possibility cannot be readily dismissed, especially if it was also possible that she somehow sublimated an unrequited natural motherhood into a possessive attachment for ornaments. Even so, Sarada Devi's choices are not fully explained in the light of Ramakrishna's ruling, for, going by available reports, Ramakrishna did not specifically insist on her wearing red bordered saris or the vermilion mark that is so prominently displayed in official photographs. For the Brahmin widow, the latter would appear to represent a greater violation of custom than wearing a gold bangle. By all appearances, she was wearing such a sari on the day she was first photographed (in 1898) at the behest of an American disciple. The vermilion mark on the forehead though is conspicuously missing and makes its appearance only in contemporary representations. Surely, this is a part of a hagiographic process, in which the Ramakrishna Mission itself is complicit. Having said that, it ought also to be admitted if the exceptional decisions that Sardamani took originated in her alone, indeed she would have to be an extremely courageous and self-willed woman to put her private fancies above the fear of social recrimination.

It would be reasonable to argue that displaying the marks of a married woman on one's person even after being widowed was a process through which the cultic strength and the acclaimed 'uniqueness' of movement around Ramakrishna was reinforced. My personal impression in the matter is that somehow the idea of an indulgent, omnipotent, omniscient spiritual figure which could alternate between the roles of a human mother and the Divine could not have been as well supported by a widow as by the woman who remained in a state of matrimony whether real or imagined. For one, Hindu mythology appears to more easily accommodate a spouseless goddess than a widowed female deity. Motherhood itself was not always contingent on marriage. In south India, we are given to understand that many village deities who go by the name of Amma (mother) are not associated with children.[9] That even as a human being she possessed extraordinary qualities of strength and endurance was a message that Sarada Devi chose to convey to her followers from time to time. In 1893, for instance, she performed the *panchatapa* penance which required sitting under the hot sun through the entire day, surrounded all around by burning fires. Narrating this experience to a devotee, she was later to point out that such performances were necessary lest people be led to think that she was only one among the ordinary.

9 Here I am referring to the article by Kamala Ganesh titled "Mother Who is Not a Mother: In Search of the Great Indian Goddess" in *Economic and Political Weekly*, 25, nos. 42–43 (20–27 October 1990). I did not however, agree with Ganesh's argument that goddesses like Kali are 'spouseless' or 'unhusbanded'. That is certainly not the understanding in ethnic Bengal.

EMERGENCE OF THE SANGHAJANANI

Swami Gambhirananda, the official historian of the Ramakrishna Math and Mission was quick to note how the Holy Mother, notwithstanding the fact that she was not a formal member of the organization and had no constitutional right to express an opinion either on its policy issues or routine activities effectively controlled the pulse of the movement. She had the power to overturn decisions taken by no less a person than Vivekananda or Swami Keshavananda of the Koalpara Ashram and her presence on some important social and religious occasion was coveted by many. She was consulted by monks even on issues concerning the guiding ideology of the movement. Once, when visiting Benares, she ruled in favour of monks being involved in social service and donated a sum of Rs 10 to the Kashi Sevashram for furthering this agenda. Sometime around 1901–02, a controversy broke out on the issue of whether or not monks of the Ramakrishna Order could count themselves as belonging to the non-dualist (Advaita) tradition of Sankara. Vivekananda, who had founded the Advaita Ashram at Mayavati in 1899 to actively pursue this ideal, was dismayed to find his brother monks resorting to the personalized worship of Ramakrishna at the ashram, quite contrary to the ideas and practices of non-dualist Vedanta. Curiously, this is reminiscent of the state of affairs that the young Debendranath Tagore (1817–1905), the spiritual successor of Rammohun Roy (1772–1833), had found upon visiting the Brahmo Samaj after Rammohun himself had departed for England. Debendranath found Brahmos openly worshipping idols and following other religious practices that were a part of orthodox Hinduism. When the matter concerning the Mayavati Ashram was put before Sarada Devi, she affirmed that the sanyasis of the Ramakrishna Order were indeed *advaitins* since their *parama guru* (the guru of gurus), Tota Puri, who had initiated Ramakrishna into *sanyas,* was a naga sanyasi belonging to this sampradaya.

Especially after Sarada's visits to Calcutta turned more frequent and even Jairambati began to regularly attract devotees and visitors from various parts of Bengal, there was a greater bonding between the nascent devotional community and the object of that devotion. Even by 1897–98, Saradamani was an important figure when it came to running the Ramakrishna Math. The land on which the Belur monastery came up was held in her name and this was a position that she later used to good advantage. When acute financial problems led Vivekananda to seriously consider selling off the land, Sarada Devi put her foot down, reminding her 'children' that since the land had been consecrated in her name, she alone had the last word in the matter. The sale was somehow stayed.

At a time when the monk disciples of Ramakrishna were scattered, unsettled and living a most frugal life in makeshift camps, there was bound to be an acute crisis in leadership. Life in these so called ashrams was uncertain, inhospitable and often, two modest meals a day were hard to come by. Some inmates did not even have an adequate change of clothes and hid themselves in dark corners when the only pair they possessed had been washed and left out in the open to dry. Jobless, devoid of any support or fixed financial backing from their larger families, most of them eked out a very humble existence and were in no position to think ahead or lead. Some others among them like Narendranath and Gangadhar Ghatak (Swami Akhandananda, 1864–1937) had already set out on their *parivrajya* or monastic tours and located at a considerable distance from Bengal. People closer at hand and placed in a relatively better position to intervene were Saradananda, Rakhal Chandra Ghosh (Swami Brahmananda, 1863–1922), Baburam (Swami Premananda, 1861–1918), Sarada Prosonno Mitra (Swami Trigunatitananda, 1865–1915) and Yogindra Nath Chaudhuri (Swami Yogananda, 1861–1919). It is important to bear in mind that of these figures, at least four were among the staunchest of Sarada's devotees and possibly contributed much to the strengthening of the cult that grew up around her. Swami Brahmananda, who was to assume the position of the first president of the Ramakrishna Mission, appears to be something of an exception. The Holy Mother found him to be troubled by recurring commonplace problems and unwilling to commit himself to their speedy resolution. His forte lay elsewhere. Brahmananda has to be among the very few direct disciples of Ramakrishna of whom we hear very little in hagiographical literature concerning Sarada.[1] Premananda, on the other hand, represented a different situation; he was much too preoccupied with the affairs of the newly founded Belur Math to spare time for other activities. That left Saradananda, Trigunatiatnanda and Yogananda, and it is to their mediating roles that we must turn when studying the early history of the Sarada cult.

In hindsight, the year 1886 would appear to mark an important watershed in the social and spiritual world of Sarada Devi for at least two reasons. The death of her husband that year was no doubt an important turning point in her life. But other events of far reaching importance also occurred around the same time. In 1886, the influential and generous Balaram Basu, whom Sarada was to call the greatest among the householder devotees of Ramakrishna, financed a pilgrim tour of north India that lasted nearly a year. The tour covered important pilgrimage sites like Baidyanath (Deoghar), Kashi, Ayodhya, Mathura-Vrindavan, Haridwar, Jaipur and Prayag. The touring party comprised at least eight

1 The biography of Brahmananda by Akshaychaitanya (*Brahmananda Lilakatha*, 2nd ed., 1965) confirms this perception. Brahmananda was overawed by the Holy Mother but failed to call on her regularly. Reportedly, he attempted to cure Sarada Devi's ailments by the use of homeopathic treatment.

people. Other than Saradamani herself, the party included Laxmimani, Golap Ma, Nikunjabala Devi, Latu, Yogindranath Raychaudhuri, Kali Prasad Chanda (Swami Abhedananda, 1866–1939) and a Brahmin widow from Dakshineswar, Kalidasi Devi. This was the first of Sarada's several pilgrim tours in the years to come. Subsequently, she visited Gaya, Bodh Gaya and Puri (November 1888–January 1889), undertook a second tour of Vrindavan (February–May 1895), visited Rameswaram, Bangalore, and some adjacent places (late 1911) and went on a third tour of Benares in 1912. In 1910, she spent over two months at Kothar in Odisha, which was a part of Balaram Basu's estate.

The first tour of 1886 is important for another reason. It was on this tour that she initiated Yogindrath Raychaudhuri who became her first disciple. Reportedly, this too was done at the behest of Ramakrishna who appeared in her visions with instructions to suitably carry out the formal initiation. On this tour, Sarada appears to have been physically fully fit. She undertook the arduous Braj Parikrama (circumambulation of the holy sites in Mathura and Vrindavan), and successfully climbed the Chandi peak at Haridwar and the Savitri tank at Pushkar. Apparently, she did not then suffer the rheumatic limp, which she was to develop later in life. Such frequent travels, often in the company of loyal devotees, had been denied to Ramakrishna himself and contributed towards making Sarada a better-known spiritual figure on a pan-Indian scale. In certain instances, her visits could be more meticulously organized and carried out given the steady institutional expansion of the Ramakrishna Math and Mission after 1898. On her tour of southern India in 1911, she was hosted by Shashi Maharaj (Swami Ramakrishnananda, 1863–1911) who ran the monastery at Madras. Sarada Devi herself worried over the fact that Ramakrishna monks still had no permanent place to settle down. In 1890, when visiting the Buddhist shrine at Bodh Gaya in the company of Swami Advaitananda she longed for a monastery where her 'children' could be permanently settled. As we know, this wish was progressively realized following Vivekananda's return from his first successful trip to the West in 1897. Generous donations from some of his Western devotees like Henrietta Muller helped purchase the land for the monastery at Belur and Sarah Bull consistently provided patronage that proved crucial for the Mission's ongoing activities. Saradamani's recurring tours contributed towards the spread of the Ramakrishna movement in upper India and elsewhere. Over time, this also led to visits to Calcutta, Jairambati and Belur by devotees from other regions of India. The first non-Bengali devotees to visit Sarada Devi in Calcutta and Jairambati sometime after 1912 were two young girls from Madras who sang Tamil bhajans at the Holy Mother's request and cooked meals the way they had been taught back home, much to Sarada Devi's delight. One of her disciples was the Parsi film actor from Bombay, Sohrab Merwanji Modi (1897–1984).

At the end of her first pilgrim tour, Sarada Devi was back in Calcutta by 31 August 1887 and was temporarily put up at Balaram Basu's residence. Hereafter followed some of the hardest days of her life, affected by poverty, neglect and loneliness. Once she moved from Calcutta to Kamarpukur, there were simply no fixed resources to fall back on. Even as she struggled to grow a few greens on the small patch of land adjoining her hut, there was no money to buy salt and other essential commodities. It was around that time that she also came to feel particularly unhappy and morose in the absence of a child of her own. On her first visit to Ramakrishna at Dakshineswar, she did express her desire to be a mother, but Ramakrishna discouraged and dismissed this as something that would only implicate him and his wife in the material world. Some of the Master's most repeated preaching and parables as reported in the *Kathamrita* revolve around the life of the hapless householder *(grihi)*, living on a paltry clerical salary, forced to live under the most unhygienic conditions with quarrelsome wives, leaking rooftops and about a dozen mouths to feed. This is a traumatic development in Sarada's life that Shyamasundari had anticipated, and she often accused her 'eccentric' son-in-law of forcing her daughter to lead such a joyless and desolate life. It is somewhat ironic though that in getting his wife to understand the travails and tragedies of human life, Ramakrishna cited the example of her own mother who had suffered several deaths at child birth. At the time, Ramakrishna's prophetic rejoinder to Shyamasundari Devi, much celebrated in hagiographic literature, was that in the days to come, her daughter would be mother to countless children. In a sense, this was an astute foretelling of Sarada's rise to the status of an extraordinary motherhood: she was the mother who was not a mother. Sarada Devi, it has to be said, quickly and gracefully came around to accept this position, even taking care to strengthen it in some ways. Arguably, her issueless state aided and consolidated her own claims to be a universal mother, a mother to both the saintly and the wicked, to the chaste and the unchaste, the pious and the impious, to honest wage earners and brigands, but even more dramatically, to both Indians and the British who were arch rivals on the political stage. This made her a somewhat unique mother-figure, ever-ready to patiently hear of the troubles that one of her children was going through and offering solace and solutions. As a widow who had actually mothered children, she might have been not very different from several women of her class who spent their lives in poverty and neglect, utterly dependent on the support of their not-too-caring and ungrateful children.

We are given to understand that it was Shyamasundari Devi who somehow prevailed upon the monks of the Ramakrishna Order to work towards some better residential arrangements for Sarada in Calcutta. In the summer of 1888, she was once again hosted by the family of Balaram Basu, after which she was forced to switch homes fairly rapidly, shuttling between Belur and Calcutta. At some point, she was put up in the close vicinity of the residence of the playwright Girish Chandra Ghosh (1844–1912), one of her best known devotees. At a garden house belonging to one Nilambar Mukhopadhyay, she camped for two successive spells between the years 1888 and 1893. Such arrangements were obviously temporary and she was forced to return to Jairambati sporadically, as between 1890–93 and 1895–97. While at Jairambati, she was visited by two of her most devoted followers, Girish Ghosh and Swami Saradananda. Girish Ghosh's calling on Sarada Devi in 1891 has some added significance for it was on this occasion that she categorically told the devotee that she was the 'real mother', not one who assumed this position by virtue of being a guru's wife, a woman addressed as 'mother' simply out of respect and politeness or even casually accepted as one. In hindsight, this appears to have coincided with her increasingly being acknowledged as a figure with divine antecedents and qualities. Sanskrit verses in her praise (*stotras*) had been composed by this time by none other than Swami Abhedananda, a direct disciple of Ramakrishna. It was also around this time that she first experienced samadhi, the state of mystical rapture that had once made Ramakrishna an object of both plain curiosity and reverence. In 1895, she left on her second tour of Benares and Vrindavan in the company of Swami Yogananda, Golap Ma and Yogin Ma.

Her movements in and out of Jairambati became less frequent after March 1898, upon returning to Calcutta yet another time. By this time, certain important developments had occurred. On 19 February 1897, Vivekananda had returned to India amidst huge rejoicing and enthusiastic public receptions. More importantly, he was accompanied by a group of Western female devotees and disciples who were keen to call on Sarada Devi of whom surely, they had heard from the Swami. This required a settled and reasonably respectable location for the Holy Mother. In March 1898, upon returning to Calcutta, Sarada Devi was put up in Baghbazar in north Calcutta, soon to be the residence also for Sister Nivedita, Vivekananda's best-known disciple. On 17 March, Nivedita in the company of the Americans Josephine McLeod (1858–1949) and Sarah Bull (1850–1911) called on Sarada Devi at her Bosepara Lane (Bagbazar) residence where she had moved in along with Golap Ma, Gopaler Ma and a few others. One of the best known public events in her life, this meeting was also groundbreaking for certain reasons. Three Western ladies (*mlecchas* in public perception) actually meeting an austere Brahmin widow in person, defying established ritual protocols, was no ordinary occurrence in itself; what was more astonishing though was the ease with which the Holy Mother agreed to share food with her guests. Evidently, Saradamani and her visitors could not make sense of each other's language and yet they understood each other in a deeper sense, through an impromptu bonding between kindred minds and souls. The Holy Mother accepted the women visitors as her 'daughters' and came to employ the Bengali word 'khuki' (a girl child) specifically for Nivedita who was also the youngest of the three. Swami Vivekananda considered this event to be no less than a miracle and Nivedita's own diary entry for the day describes it as 'a day of days'. On 7 April 1899, the three ladies met Sarada Devi once again, formally welcoming her on her maiden visit to Belur where construction work for the new monastery had begun. It pleased the Holy Mother immensely that the 'boys' were about to have something that they could truly call their own.

Meetings between the three ladies and Sarada Devi was also immortalized by the fact that in November that year, a European photographer by the name of Harrington was engaged by Sarah Bull to take photographs of

Sarada Devi. This is a proposal to which she consented after much reluctance. Two successive photographs of her were taken on the day with the Holy Mother seated in slightly different postures. By some curious coincidence, both Ramakrishna and Sarada Devi were photographed around the age of 45, in 1883 and 1898 respectively. It somehow did not occur to Sarah Bull to have themselves photographed with the Mother and it is reasonable to argue that at the time, insisting on a group photograph might have looked quite demanding and disrespectful to the European and American devotees. That would have been ascending two steps at a time and rather rapidly. After all, as Ramakrishna's spouse, Sarada Devi was placed even above their own guru, Swami Vivekananda. The only exception to this was the well-known photograph of Nivedita in the company of the Mother, the two women looking at each other with awe and affection. Of Josephine McLeod and Sarah Bull, we catch sight either in American photographs or else when photographed in the company of Swami Vivekananda.

By one estimate, Sarada Devi was photographed at least 40 times, in her lifetime, the last of these were taken when travelling from Vishnupur to Calcutta in 1920. She was also photographed twice following her death.

Photographs of the Holy Mother were not circulated for a long time. Sarah Bull herself had comforted her with the assurance that the photograph would be distributed only among American devotees. On 4 January 1899, Nivedita—writing to Mrs Hammond, wife of an English disciple of Vivekananda by the name of Eric Hammond—had to reiterate that the photographs were meant for private circulation only. It was roughly three years later in 1902 that Eric Hammond, writing for *The Theosophical Review* made the news public knowledge. Even so, in India itself, her photographs became accessible only a few months before her death in 1920. One of Saradamani's devotees who first met her in 1917, later recalled that neither a biography of her nor a photograph was available at the time. It is during the last 10 years of Sarada's life that the number of devotees and disciples swelled considerably, some of whom would have been keen to add a photograph to their collection of memorabilia. Until that time, however, no person who was not an initiated disciple had access to these. There was an air of closely-guarded secrecy about it all. This is borne out by the testimony from Swami Gambhirananda: 'When we were young,' the swami admits, 'we never spoke publicly about the Holy

Mother...it was important that she be kept out of pubic gaze since the public would not understand her." Swami Saradananda discouraged a devotee by the name of Labanyakumar Chakrabarty from publishing a biography of Sarada that he was working on. Over time, however, such concerns for privacy was clearly outweighed by the publicity that marketable photographs could bring to a fast expanding cult and an emerging cult leader. Sarada Devi acknowledged this herself. Speaking of the value that circulated photographs added to the propagation of the Ramakrishna cult she was to observe:

> Oh! How clever the people of Calcutta have turned out to be! They managed to photograph the Master several times and *Master Moshai* (Mahendranath Gupta) carefully jotted down every word that the Master had uttered. Of which previous avatar have photographs been taken or words so meticulously memorialized?

During 1898–99, the Holy Mother contributed substantially towards further popularizing the Ramakrishna cult. The *Kathamrita* volumes of Mahendranath Gupta that took the bhadralok world of Calcutta by storm were yet to arrive and plans for setting up a monastery at Belur for monks of the Ramakrishna Order was coming up tardily, brick by brick. Sarada Devi on the other hand, took it upon herself to project her husband as a veritable god-man at select but symbolically significant places. She unveiled a photograph of Ramakrishna and conducted a formal worship twice in quick succession on 12 November 1898 at Belur and in March 1899 in the Bagbazar area of north Calcutta where Nivedita and a few other prominent devotees lived. On 24 February 1901, Ramakrishna's birthday celebrations were held at Belur, followed by the autumnal Durga Puja at the behest of Swami Vivekananda. It is generally believed that this tactically brilliant event helped the local Hindu population to overlook the ritual transgressions that the Swami had committed, first in attempting to act as the representative of Hinduism despite being a non-Brahmin, and second, his crossing the seas and allegedly partaking "un-Hindu" food on occasions. Here it may be recalled that in 1897, upon his return to India, he was denied entry to the Dakshineswar premises on precisely these charges. In 1907, the Holy Mother attended a private Durga Puja celebration at the residence of the playwright Girish

Ghosh, which considerably added to her charisma and popularity in the area; in all probability, this was the first occasion when some reputable actresses of the Bengali stage like Teenkori and Tarasundari were added to the list of her acquaintances. As we shall presently see, she had a special gift for endearing herself to socially marginalized men and women. In 1909, she organized Ramakrishna's birthday celebrations at Kamarpukur itself, thereby allowing the cult to penetrate the heart of rural Bengal.

Through these years, the organizational strength of the Ramakrishna movement increased with Sarada remaining as its nucleus. From this perspective too, it was important that allowances be made for constructing a permanent place of residence for her in Calcutta. In 1906, a local business man by the name of Kedar Das, having made some windfall profits in business, gifted a small plot of land to the monks in north Calcutta and this encouraged Swami Saradananda to arrange for a loan of Rs 57,000, mostly collected from devotees, for construction purposes. A small strip of land adjacent to this plot was later added to this so as to make the living quarters more airy and spacious. A sum of little over Rs 11,000 were spent on constructing what eventually came to be called Matri Mandir (the Mother's Abode) and was perhaps the first major public acknowledgement of the charisma that Sarada Devi had come to acquire by then. On 23 May 1909, she formally stepped into the newly constructed building that was to serve as her permanent residential quarters in Calcutta for the next eleven years. She lived on the upper floor with a fairly large retinue comprising Golap Ma, Radhu, Yogin Ma and other close female devotees. The lower floor served as the office for the journal *Udbodhan* (started 1899) and where the man of corpulent frame, the veteran Swami Saradananda, who described himself as the "Mother's doorkeeper" lived and assiduously worked. Saradananda himself regulated the thick flow of devotees and disciples who thronged the Udbodhan office day and night until it became necessary to impose further restrictions. Eventually, male visitors were allowed to meet the Mother (whenever in residence) only on Tuesdays and Saturdays. At other times, as several devotees have noted, she was virtually surrounded by women of all ages, making it difficult for even monks of the Ramakrishna Order to approach her. Sarada Devi would never venture to travel to Calcutta unless she knew Saradananda to be around. Saradananda was vital to her life and activities both at Jairambati and in Calcutta. It was he who intervened a second time in 1915, when differences between her brothers erupted again, on this occasion on an even more serious note. Separate quarters for her had to be built at Jairambati in 1916 and at the adjacent Koalpara ashram, which she occasionally visited. Saradananda, it may be recalled, was also the main conduit through whom donations coming from Vivekananda's American and English disciples reached Calcutta, as for instance, the monthly sum of Rs 60, which Sarah Bill paid lifelong until her death in 1911. We know from accounts left by one of Sarada's householder devotees and biographer, Ashutosh Mitra, that Vivekananda himself arranged for a monthly payment of Rs 25 and there was irregular assistance from Girish Ghosh. Hereafter, whenever residing at Jairambati, she was assured of a monthly income of Rs 35, of which Rs 10 each were paid by Mahendranath Gupta, Lalit Chattopadhyay and the mother of the nationalist leader, Surendranath Banerjee (1848–1925). The rest was paid by Sarada Prosonno Mitra (Swami Trigunatitananda). Other than paying the monthly sum of Rs 10, Mahendranath Gupta helped her financially on several occasions. He contributed towards the construction of the separate quarters for her at Jairambati and gifted a substantial quantity of gold ornaments to Sarada's niece, Radhu, on the occasion of her marriage. Perhaps more than anyone else, the Holy Mother was aware of the material success that 'Mastermoshai' (Mahendranath Gupta) had procured through the sale proceeds of the *Kathamrita*. As Sarada recalled, the man could pay a sum of only Rs 2 as long as he was a school teacher.

Ill health dogged Sarada Devi for the most of her life. Sometime after her return from the tour of north India in 1886, she developed painful rheumatism in the left leg with the result that she had to keep it stretched when squatting on the ground. Although various cures were tried, nothing brought her lasting relief. Whenever at Dakshineswar, she suffered from acute dysentery, as did her husband, and this continued even during her days at the Matrimandir. In 1909, when in Calcutta, she was diagnosed with chicken pox and the infection spread to Golap Ma, who was slower to recover. However, most of all she suffered from recurring malarial attacks in Jairambati and Kamarpurkur, which left her greatly emaciated. This, as it may be recalled, had caused an enlarged spleen, which she had to be rather painfully cured of, in the native way, by applying burning wood to the affected spot.

Signs of acute illness were first reported in 1918, shortly after her birthday celebrations that year while she was at Jairambati. A team of doctors attended on her even at the time. But the fever kept returning and she was moved to Calcutta where she underwent a variety of treatments including allopathic, homeopathy and Ayurveda. Nothing seemed to work and it was only in May 1920, only a couple of months prior to her death that Dr Prandhan Basu diagnosed her for kala azar, effective treatment for which was available only after 1929. It is somewhat ironical that during the last 10 years of her life, Sarada rose to the status of an undisputed cult leader, the 'highest court of appeal' in all matters as Taraknath Ghoshal (Swami Sivananda) was to put it, she continually suffered from the twin effects of ill health and bereavement. The former wore her down bodily and the second sapped her mental strength. The first shocks of bereavement came in 1898–99, when Swami Yogananda and her youngest brother, Abhayacharan, died within a few months of each other. The first she compared to bricks being cast off a monument: admittedly, Yogananda and Saradananda were her most zealous and caring devotees. In 1902, Vivekananda passed away while she was away at Jairambati and though her reactions to the event are not recorded, it is reasonable to surmise that she bemoaned the death of someone who was Ramakrishna's 'special instrument of play' and who himself had made his guru a globally respected name. Successive bereavements rocked her own family during 1905–06: uncle Nilmadhav passing away in 1905, Shymasundari Devi in 1906 and brother Prasannakumar losing his first wife that year. In 1911, she lost in quick succession Shashi (Swami Ramkrishnananda, her host at Madras) and Nivedita to hill dysentery at the hilly retreat of Darjeeling. In a second wave of successive deaths that occurred between 1918 and 1920, she lost swamis Premananda and Adbhutananda, and finally, another brother, Baradaprasanna. Her persistent attachments in life, as for instance, to her nieces Radhu, Nalini or Sushila, were dramatically cast off as the end approached. Radhu was a particularly traumatic case. There was a time when sleep would not come to Saradamani unless she had Radhu beside her in bed; towards the end though, she sternly and surprisingly severed her relations, asking her devotees to take her away to Jairambati. By mid-July of the year 1920, she had a premonition of imminent death and somewhat wistfully told Sharat (Saradananda) that she was leaving the flock to his care. On 16 July, she reportedly advised a female devotee thus:

> Speak ill of no one, my child. Seek your own blemishes if you have to. Learn to make this world your own. This world belongs to you. There is really no one whom you cannot count among your own.

These are not sentiments that she may have abruptly come upon on her death bed. In a sense, they also reflect her thoughts and social experiences. In her everyday life, she rarely practised any form of discrimination, not even against those for whom such discrimination had come to be accepted as common social practice. Oddly, her liberality manifested itself more within the decidedly conservative rural setting of Jairambati and not cosmopolitan Calcutta. Amidst the bhadralok society of Calcutta, she was constrained to behave in a decorous way and to artfully play certain roles assigned to her. Back in Jairambati, she was somebody's sister, an aunt, a mother or even a daughter who could fall back on childhood days with greater nostalgia and freedom. Swami Prabhavananda has noted that at Jairambati, she did not scruple to even sport a veil, which stifled her in the presence of the often-pretentious society of genteel Calcutta. In itself, this serves as an apt reminder of the complex dynamics of everyday social relationships that often worked in inscrutable ways.

She died a little past midnight on 21 July 1920. The body was carried by boat all the way to Belur where she was duly cremated. On 21 December 1921, coinciding with her 68th birthday, monks and lay devotees contributed to laying the foundation stone to a new shrine (also called Matri Mandir) in her honour. The shrine dedicated to her now stands alongside that of her 'eccentric' husband and that of the monk who had once taken the world by storm. Devotees and visitors travelling to the popular shrine at Jairambati cannot but notice the presence of the 'Mother' sprawling across the azure sky.

MOTHERHOOD: HUMAN AND DIVINE

A distinctive feature in the life of Sarada Devi was the ability to effectively alternate between playing out the roles of human mother and the Divine, even to the extent of subtly blending the two. As early as 1898, an anonymous writer writing in *The Literary Digest of New York* could claim that people 'regarded her as the personified divine Motherhood and the embodiment of chastity, purity and spirituality.' Evidently, our author understood Sarada as both the devotee as well as the object of human devotion. In other comparable cases, as say with Nirmala Sundari Chakraborty (Anandamayi Ma, 1896–1982), one of these identities appears to have decidedly outweighed the other in public perception. Whereas, with the devotees and disciples of Sarada Devi, there was a sense of joyous abandon and emotional fulfillment in the company of a mother-like figure, in the case of Anandamayi Ma, the 'ananda' (joy permeated state) was clearly on the side of an ineffable spiritual ecstasy. Saradamani did not sermonize or hold public discourses, grant formal interviews, lead religious gatherings or preside over long sessions of rapturous devotional singing. The Sarada Math, the monastery for women named after her, came into existence long after her time and this was also not an idea in which she had expressed any interest herself. A permanent residential site of the monks of the Ramakrishna Order, her homeless 'children' was what she coveted more. She lacked the wit, repertoire, communication skills and the social charisma of her husband, Sri Ramakrishna. She also went without the benefit of being served by as illustrious a disciple as Vivekananda who placed the Ramakrishna cult on a global footing and the services of meticulous archivist in Mahendranath Gupta who so enduringly canonized the preaching and parables of the Master. At least in her lifetime, Sarada Devi did not receive the attention of various contemporary religious groups in Bengal, as for instance, the Brahmos, Vaishnava evangelists or orthodox pundits to the extent her husband did. Also, she was never as celebrated in the Bengali language press. Unlike Ramakrishna, or for that matter even some of her own spiritual companions like

Gauri Ma or Yogin Ma, she was not as widely travelled or trained in spiritual praxis and experimentation (*sadhana*). Taken together, these factors defy a ready explanation for the reverence and great popularity that she came to enjoy in her lifetime and more so thereafter.

It would be natural to presume that the 'divine' antecedents of Sarada came to be recognized later in time, only after she assumed the status of a cultic leader, following the death of her husband. However, a closer look at our sources suggests otherwise. Even when the couple was stationed at Dakshineswar, between the years 1872 and 1886, with intervening gaps in time, Sri Ramakrishna would make repeated references to her divine origins, affirming her identity with Saraswati, the goddess of learning. Once at Kamarpukur, he was not disappointed to find that his child bride had fallen asleep while he busied himself with his religious discourses before a gathering of local women. "Let her be," he had gently said, "for if she were to hear and truly register such spiritual talk, she would awaken to her true identity and then it might prove hard to keep her tied to worldly life." He also warned his nephew Hriday Mukhopadhyay, who is known to have occasionally treated Sarada Devi with some indifference and disrespect, to desist from such behaviour. Ramakrishna feared that if she were to be somehow offended, his own spiritual practices would come to naught. The man also depended greatly on his wife for certain routine services that she dutifully and diligently rendered. One of these was to take care of his special dietary needs.[1] During his last days when he had been afflicted by cancer of the throat and had to be moved to various places in Calcutta for better medical care, Ramakrishna came to depend on her services even more. When living in one of these makeshift homes, Sarada Devi accidentally injured her foot and could not attend to the needs of her husband. This made Ramakrishna panic, but the man also had the good humour to ask one of his disciples, Swami Premananda, if he could manage to carry her about in a basket, much to the amusement of all present! Whether

1 The historian and biographer Narasingha Sil believes Ramakrishna to be affected by a food fetish and thus making unreasonable demands on his wife. There is reason to believe though that Sarada Devi was herself not a particularly accomplished cook. Once at Kamarpukur, having tasted a dish cooked by her, Ramakrishna compared her to the quack in relation to a certified physician. Upon this, Hriday Mukhopadhyay, who was present on the occasion, quipped that while the quack would be available at even short notice and his services could be counted upon any time, the certified physician was bound to be less approachable. Ramakrishna is known to have agreed to this wholeheartedly.

or not for purely functional needs. Sri Ramakrishna did seriously try to take good care of his wife; her husband would not bear the thought of hurting her even with the stroke of a flower, Saradamani once told a disciple.

Even at a time when her spiritual powers had come to be acknowledged, it was the human side to her motherhood that was highlighted in contemporary accounts. Swami Prabhavananda (1893–1976), long associated with the Vedanta Society of South California, recalled how to everyone who met her, she looked like one's own mother and how she conducted herself in ways peculiarly associated with motherly care and concern. Regardless of her own material state or the social environment in which she was located, Sarada Devi was consistently associated with the ideas of feeding, nurturing and more generally with affectionate care, born of endearing maternal instincts. Cooks and casual visitors have both testified to the fact that somehow she seemed to know just what choices her 'children' would make by way of a fixing a menu or just what would suit each of them. In her early days at Dakshineswar, her pampering, motherly instincts resisted the dietary regime that Sri Ramakrishna himself had imposed on some of his devotees and disciples. Whereas

Ramakrishna had insisted that the young men aspiring to be monks adapt themselves to a life of hardship, his wife complained that a mother's instincts would never agree to treat her children thus. This was almost a leaf taken out of a favourite parable of Ramakrishna himself which spoke of the 'all knowing mother' who knew how to vary her dishes, in keeping with the varying tastes and dispositions of her several children. Reportedly, she would sit by her guests at meal time, asking then pointedly if a special dish had been cooked the right way or if they had eaten to their heart's content, just as a mother typically would. She also insisted on herself clearing the leaf-plates left behind after the meal, again very much like a mother routinely would. That she carried out motherly duties at considerable trouble to herself and generally amidst a life of denial and poverty was not hidden from her devotees and might have endeared her to them all the more. As a person, she looked so plain and ordinary that many men and women, later associated with the Ramakrishna-Sarada movement, were far from impressed in their very first meeting with the Holy Mother. Parul Mukhopadhyay (later Pravrajika Bharatiprana, 1894–1973) the first president of the Sarada Math, met her when eight years old and came away rather disappointed. At Benares, the more outspoken and imposing figure of Golap Ma was once mistaken for that of Sarada. Swami Satswarupananda, originally a schoolteacher from Katihar, who first met her in the year 1919, long fought the idea that she had claims to some divine qualities.

In some scholarly studies of Sarada Devi, ascriptions of motherhood have been sought to be explained in somewhat reductionist terms. Narasingha P. Sil, the author of perhaps the only critical study of Sarada to date, puts this down to certain crafty manipulation employed by monks of the Ramakrishna Order, no less by Vivekananda himself. We are given to understand that Sarada became a natural choice once Ramakrishna himself had departed, leaving a visible vacuum in leadership. Sil argues that Vivekananda was especially persuaded to uphold the idea of a woman spiritual successor to Ramakrishna, impressed as he was at witnessing the social and professional progress that women had made in the West and by the pressing need for reforming the status of Indian women. Some scholars of the Ramakrishna Order have expanded upon this idea to suggest that Ramakrishna's locating motherhood in God itself paved the way for the emancipation of Indian women. In 1894, Vivekananda, then on his missionary tours of America, wrote home to a brother disciple suggesting that the importance of even Ramakrishna himself would fade before that of the Holy Mother. Sil also argues that valourizing motherhood, whether human or divine, was distinctive to Hindu Bengali culture and hence, ascriptions of Divine Motherhood upon somebody who was in any case basking in some reflected glory cast by her god-man husband, was by no means as outlandish as would prima facie appear. From this emanates the further argument that playing out the role of a mother to all worked as some kind of a compensatory mechanism for a woman who was denied children of her own. It was thus that an unrequited natural motherhood that Saradamani certainly aspired was apotheosized into a universal motherhood.

The question as to why Sarada accepted such a life for herself has been answered in two different ways. Monk-biographers of Sarada Devi, as for instance, swamis Gambhirananda and Nikhilananda, have argued that Sri Ramakrishna did offer his wife a free choice in the matter, which she then resolved by selflessly choosing not to act as an impediment to her husband's spiritual life. Biographies of this genre especially report

Ramakrishna's pointedly asking his wife if she intended to 'drag back' her husband into mundane *samsaric* (worldly) life and with the devoted and understanding wife promptly replying in the negative. There is no reason to doubt that Sarada Devi counted upon experiencing a normal conjugal life, to be blessed by children of her own and mothering them into a healthy adulthood. Reportedly, it was only after some cajoling from her husband, which Sil interprets as 'veiled threats' held out by him, that she reluctantly gave up such desires. We read also of Ramakrishna's putting into her the fear of withstanding repeated pain and traumatic bereavement that would follow from some of her children dying at childbirth, only to be rebuffed by Sarada retorting that it was unlikely that all her children would so die! There is every reason to believe, therefore, that if Sarada Devi agreed to remain out of a conjugal life, she did so with feelings of anguished reluctance. Contemporaries of Ramakrishna, as for instance, the Brahmo theologian Protap Chandra Mozumdar (1840–1905) had accused the saint of treating his wife with some 'barbarity' and evidently, they had in mind his reluctance to be drawn into a normal conjugal life. This charge, as we know, was denied by two of Sri Ramakrishna's oldest biographers:

Max Muller and Romain Rolland, both of whom cited Sarada Devi's own denial of any 'barbaric treatment'. It is a reasonable guess that they would have gathered this information from either Swami Vivekananda or else Saradananda, both of whom were in correspondence with these Western biographers. Writing closer to our time, Dinesh Chandra Dasgupta (Swami Nikhilananda, 1895–1973) of the Vedanta Society of New York, has put this down to the fanciful reading of a holy Hindu life by a Westernized, ultra reformist body, the Brahmo Samaj.

It is not clear to us just what ultimately prevailed upon Saradamani to accept her fate as an issueless woman. Did Ramakrishna reveal to her (as he apparently did before some of his other male acquaintances like the Brahmo evangelist, Sibnath Sastri) his loss of erotic urges or his allegedly homoerotic tendencies which, according to scholars like Jeffrey Kripal, would have prevented a healthy bisexual relationship? In explaining Ramakrishna's reluctance to be drawn into a conjugal life, Sil appears to also work upon an older argument offered by the revolutionary nationalist and a practising tantric, Motilal Roy (1883–1959), that their unnatural difference in age prevented Ramakrishna form developing a sexual interest in his wife. Sil's own understanding though gravitates more upon the 'plain' looks of Sarada, which allegedly failed to arouse her husband.

It is equally unclear if even early in her married life, Sarada Devi had come to realize that by leading a life of austere chastity she would eventually emerge as the embodiment of the ideal Indian woman and universal mother as some of her monastic and lay devotees have somewhat pompously apotheosized. In all likelihood, this was a status that weighed with her later in life as a part as an irreversible condition and to which she had to be sufficiently reconciled. It does also seem reasonable to argue that any 'manipulative' strategy employed by Sri Ramakrishna to force a life of celibacy upon his wife has to be read alongside Sarada's own growing awareness of her charismatic value to the movement. Apparently, at some point in time, she herself came to believe in claims made about her exalted and extraordinary qualities or powers. Speaking of hagiographic functions, one cannot but notice the uncanny resemblance between the apocryphal stories narrated about Saradamani's birth and that of Ramakrishna. In both instances, the mothers, Shyamasundari Devi and Chandramani Devi respectively, felt some divine power entering their wombs prior to child birth. Sarada Devi's claims to a divine status, as I shall argue, were no less the result of her own self-understanding and discursive projections.

Sarada Devi's emergence 'as a mother to all', marked as it was by a humanly protective motherly instinct, is relatively easier to follow and document. Here it is important to remember that within her role as a 'mother', Sarada Devi also carried functions of a trusted social and spiritual counsellor. She offered advice to barren wives, estranged husbands, young men neglected or disowned by their families, students caught in two minds on whether to marry, political workers hounded by the police or people simply afflicted by ill health and poverty. Arguably, this was a role that Ramakrishna too had played to the hilt, offering solace and some practicable solutions to people from various walks of life, troubled as they were by new forms of duress in a world of sharpening polarities and rapidly shrinking opportunities. But in addition, Sarada Devi also offered easy initiation to people affected by a spiritual angst and but for rare exceptions, she never turned down a seeker. By all accounts, the process of initiation was a simple affair, lasting barely a few minutes and yet had a lasting psychological effect on those initiated. People so initiated were given to understand that they had been freed of their follies and sins and would in all probability be spared even a rebirth. They were also assured that in times of difficulty or distress, they would have a benignly caring mother to fall back on. The important point here is that in so holding out hopes of relief and redemption, not only did Sarada Devi refuse to make any exceptions based on caste, community or gender, but at times naively overlooked the obvious. Thus, even in the Swadeshi years when Bengal was rocked by a rapidly intensifying anti-colonial agitation, she counted Englishmen and Indians alike as her children and expected them to amicably patch up their differences. She preferred purchasing finer imported cloth for women in her ashrams over the coarser variety produced by local looms, even in the face of some disappointment and opposition. The quarrel that political volunteers had with the colonial police or the administration, as she understood it, was best sorted out between the concerned parties without motherly love being forced to make arbitrary choices between her sons. Ramakrishna himself feared the figure of the white European, whether in the form of the baton yielding, beefy policeman or the boss in government offices who terrorized petty Indian clerks;[2] his wife apparently, had no such inhibitions. Sarada's freely violating ritual norms in respect of low-caste Hindus, Muslims or men and women of 'disreputable' character stands in some contrast to her husband's exercising far greater restraint and reluctance precisely in respect of such social categories. Sarada would at times defy her husband's advice to desist from keeping the company of some 'fallen' woman that she simply could not turn down someone who looked upon her as mother. Nor did she give in to the wishes of Krishnabhavini Dasi, wife of the Ramakrishna patron, Balaram Basu, that she stop hosting a certain woman who carried a blot on her character. Motherly affection, in her understanding, overruled such exceptions.

In some instances, however, the idea of the ubiquitous mother has come to be associated with some unlikely forms. It has been argued that in keeping with the nationalist rhetoric of the times, Vivekananda constructed Sarada Devi in the image of 'Mother of India'.[3] For a man who was keen to dissociate the newly

2 Ramakrishna enjoyed the novelist Bankimchandra's once quipping that it was kicks from the white master's boots that had bent his body at places and hence earned the name 'Bankim' (literally, bent).

3 This is further discussed in "Sarada Devi: A Reappraisal".

founded Ramakrishna Math and Mission from political activities so as to avoid police surveillance, this would have been an unlikely thing to do. Neither Vivekananda nor his favoured pupil, Nivedita, would have fancied the figure of Sarada as something even faintly resembling Bharat Mata, an icon that really came to the fore a few years after the passing of Vivekananda in 1902. For one, they would have both preferred to see her as a sanitized, spiritual figure which embodied not active or assertive political energy but quiescent, self-negating renunciation. For them, renouncing the self was the first step to forming the national collective.

Speaking from hindsight, ascriptions of her divine status may be said to have originated in three distinct yet interrelated sources: in Sri Ramakrishna, in devotees and disciples associated with the Ramakrishna Order, but no less in Sarada Devi herself. Of these, the first has already been briefly examined; this was a factor which ran like a subterranean stream, invisible at times and yet acutely potent all along. But to now speak of the two other sources. All her life, Saradamani projected herself as a loyal wife and devotee of Ramakrishna, and very often, her advice to people affected by some personal or social crisis was simply to pray to him for relief.

Another persistent habit with her was to affirm that she was but an instrument in her godly husband's, hands as was 'Naren', more famously, Swami Vivekananda. However, this did not belittle her power and potency. She fully believed that she had been entrusted to carry out Sri Ramakrishna's will and to practically execute his merciful designs for redeeming the world. Such self-understanding soon came to be supported by a growing belief in her extraordinary status or powers. One of the earliest to proclaim her divine status was the wife of Ramakrishna's influential and affluent patron, Sambhu Mallik. This tradition has carried over time. Parivrajika Muktiprana of the Sarada Math and a biographer of the Holy Mother, considers Saradamani to be the first and foremost of all Ramakrishna devotees. Such ideas may have been floated not long after Ramakrishna's death in 1886, but especially caught on after 1891. There are two related reasons for arguing thus. That year, on his first visit to Jairambati, the actor and playwright Girish Ghosh was startled upon catching sight of the Holy Mother since hers was the very face that had earlier appeared in his dreams, offering an ailing man loving benediction that had the power and assurance to cure. No less significantly, on 10 November of that year,

Sarada Devi personally participated in the Jagaddhatri Puja at Jairambati. Possibly, this contributed to a subtle overlapping of the two roles, human and the Divine, that she was to play out in the years to come. We have it on the authority of Ashutosh Mitra, a lay biographer of Sarada Devi, that an ornate worship of the Holy Mother was organized in the year 1903 by her devotees. At the Kothar Ashram in Odisha, she permitted one Surendranath Sarkar to ritually worship her with flowers. Before another, she displayed the *abhayamudra*, a sign traditionally associated with a deity exuding grace and holding out hopes of redemption.

Visitors who called on Sarada Devi whether at Jairambati or else at the Udbodhan office in Calcutta mostly sought relief from recurring, commonplace problems. The belief that a quasi-Divine figure had the power to heal both the mind and the body of loyal devotees perceptibly grew into a matter of faith. Such beliefs would have carried far in social circles with a well-known figure like Girish Ghosh actively propagating it. In 1907, despite protracted illness, Sarada Devi travelled all the way from Jairambati to Bagbazar in north Calcutta to attend a private Durga Puja held in the Ghosh residence. Other than

Girish Ghosh himself, Nitya Niranjan Ghosh (Swami Niranjanananda, d.1904) and Durgacharan Nag (1846–99) were two other disciples of Ramakrishna who contributed substantially to the propagation of the Sarada cult. The fanatically devoted Durgacharan Nag, popularly called Nag Mahashay, would repeatedly bang his head on the door jamb leading to Sarada Devi's room at Udbodhan to announce his arrival and even chew on the leaf plate on which was served the *prasad* offered by the Holy Mother. Swamis Yogananda and Premananda were visibly irritated at people who did not hold Sarada Devi at par with her husband. As we know, the Holy Mother herself labelled Yogin and Sharat (Saradananda) as her most dedicated servitors. Until his untimely death in 1899, Yogananda was a full-time attendant and caretaker for Sarada Devi, also accompanying her on several pilgrim tours. Swami Trigunatitananda, once travelling to Jairambati in the company of the Holy Mother, hurriedly alighted from the bullock cart carrying them to lay himself down upon a ditch on the path so that the cart could smoothly pass over the ditch without causing much discomfort to her. Saradananda, apart from being the 'Mother's doorkeeper' at Udbodhan and rescuing her often in moments of financial and family crisis, was also instrumental in popularizing the idea that the Holy Mother could by no means be a common woman. 'Do you seriously think that God (meaning Ramakrishna) chose to take for his wife the daughter of a woman who collected cow-dung for a living?'—he had once indignantly asked a Ramakrishna devotee. To Saradananda, we also owe the idea typically articulated in his well-known work, *Bharate Shakti Puja*, Part 1 (1911) that worshipping woman as mother was a distinctive feature of Indian faith systems. Apart from being drawn from a variety of textual sources, such thoughts also powerfully echo the thoughts of Vivekananda himself. In his lectures delivered in America and in his correspondence with Western disciples, Vivekananda argued that in India, it was the mother who was idealized, never the wife. In the closing years of his life, it was the comforting thought of the kindly, indulgent and all-forgiving mother that led the Swami to exhibit a child-like reversion in a manner that again collapsed the divide between the human and the divine. In 1897, on a tour of the Kshir Bhavani shrine in Kashmir, the Swami had felt justly chastised by the words of the Divine Mother, which came across the skies: 'It is all Mother now', as Nivedita reported the Swami saying in her classic, *The Master as I Saw Him*, '…Mother said what if unbelievers should enter my temple and defile my image, what is that to you? Do you protect me or do I protect you?' Once repulsed by the 'hideous' sight of the ferocious, blood-thirsty deity Kali, Vivekananda, in his last years, wrote poems to Kali, goaded Nivedita to publicly lecture on the goddess, so as to counter the iconoclastic Brahmos and for a man who had consistently upheld the value of human initiatives surprisingly pointed to its very worthlessness before Divine Will. For Vivekananda, the Holy Mother was a subtle combination of the human and the Divine. The Swami once described her as the 'living goddess' (*jiyanta* Durga). To a brother monk, Swami Sivananda (Taraknath Ghosal), Vivekananda observed how while Ramakrishna's status as an avatar could be a matter of debate, those who did not revere the Holy Mother had cause to feel ashamed. In Sarada Devi, he also appears to have found powerful cultural and social symbols integral to Hinduism: womanly austerity and the spirit of selfless renunciation; it was the purity and chastity of the Hindu widow on which rested the strength and sanctity of an ideal Hindu society. The Swami sought the Holy Mother's blessings each time he went abroad, in 1893 and 1899, and was also the first to insist on the idea of founding a separate monastic organization for women. Evidently, he was impressed by her willingness to endure personal hardship for a larger cause, her unflinching loyalty towards her husband who was his spiritual guru and the openness and liberality that an orthodox Brahmin woman showed to Western devotees in a manner that defied all established conventions. What might have specially moved him the most was the potentiality, visible even within traditionally orthodox society, to move and relocate itself within vortices of progressive change. Despite some of his innate conservatism regarding the status of the Hindu wife and widow, Swami Vivekananda was strongly on the side of ameliorating the status of the Indian woman, giving her education, dignity and a voice to speak up for herself. In modern India, he would have to be perhaps the only Hindu thinker to have argued that women needed to be granted agency and that they could themselves best solve their own problems.

In a slim and relatively unknown work, *Sri Sri Sarada Mahima* (1997), Swami Prabhananda, the historian of the Ramakrishna movement, has revealed to us interesting details of how, especially following the Sarada Centenary Year (1953), repeated attempts have been made to theologize Sarada Devi and to situate her within the framework of classical Sanskrit poetic conventions. The earliest attempt to compose adulatory Sanskrit verses (*stotra*) in her honour goes back to the year 1888, when Kali Prasad Chanda (Swami Abhedananda) narrated some *stotra*s before the Holy Mother and won her praise and blessings. Sarada Devi was formally worshipped in the manner Ramakrishna himself was, but in her own lifetime itself. The first such event occurred at the Alambazar Math in 1897. Ashutosh Mitra further claims that she was worshipped alongside the goddess on the occasion of Durga Puja celebrations of 1903. On 16 October 1912, as she stopped at the gates of Belur, the monks, freeing the horse from the carriage, pulled it themselves all the way to the main shrine. In the history of the Ramakrishna movement, she was the only person other than Vivekananda, to have been bestowed this honour.[4] In 1916 again, on a similar occasion, she was thronged by a swelling crowd of men

4 This occurred in 1897 upon the Swami's triumphant return to Calcutta on completing his historic tour of the West.

and women who kept persisting for her blessings by reverentially touching her feet, much to her discomfort. Abhedananda's attempts at composing Sanskrit *stotra*s were followed by those of Swami Gunatitananda, who went a step further by creatively borrowing from the *dhyanmantra* dedicated to the goddess Shodashi (Tripurasundari), whose divine presence Ramakrishna had once located and celebrated in Sarada. In 1988, a collection of 1,000 verses known as *Sri Sarada Sahasranama* composed by Swami Apurvananda, a personal disciple of the Holy Mother, was formally adopted by certain branches of the Ramakrishna Math. This was followed by another collection authored by Swami Harshananda, which reportedly set even 'higher standards' in literary composition. Swami Prabhananda makes it a point to remind us that the name 'Sarada' or 'Saraswati' was one of the thousand names conferred on the Great Goddess in the work, *Lalitasahasranama*, and that in the *Bhavani-Nama-Sahasrastuti*, she is also called Khemankari, the name originally conferred on infant Sarada. In our author's perception, evidently, these could not be dismissed as mere coincidence. One of her Western devotees, Laura Glenn (Sister Devmata, 1867–1942), who regularly called on the Holy Mother at her Bagbazar residence and almost reverentially tidied up her bed every morning, was to later observe how 'the human cover in her was too thin to hide the radiance of divine consciousness beneath.'

Narasingha Sil aptly identifies Sarada Devi herself to be a major source of hagiographic literature that grew up around her. Most of these were in the nature of self-conscious confessions narrated before devotees and disciples, which were then replicated in numerous biographical works. She unabashedly told Swami Tapasyananda (1904–91), a disciple of Swami Sivananda who later rose to be the Vice President of the Ramakrishna Math and Mission, that if Ramakrishna was Bhagavan, she herself had to be Bhagavati. Before Swami Kesavanada of the Koalpara Ashram, she affirmed that she was the Great Goddess of whom folk deities like Shasthi and Shitala were but minor parts. When Swami Ishanananda asked her how even an incipient awareness of her divine status allowed her to carry on with daily chores, she suggested that such awareness was purposively cast aside since that would come in the way of performing her routine domestic functions. To another unidentifiable devotee, she is known to have said the following:

> People call me Divine Mother. I think maybe they are right. How else can one explain the strange things that have happened in my life.

At times, she made statements that would have sounded jolting if only for their lack of historicity. On one of her several visits to Benares upon spotting a group of Western tourists at Sarnath, she remarked that those had once built the *stupa*s and other artifacts had returned to inspect their work! Inside the shrine at Rameswaram in 1911, she looked at the *linga* and wistfully observed how it had remained rooted to the spot where she had once placed it! However, having pronounced the claim and then realizing its very brazenness she hurriedly retracted by suggesting that that she had said so in a fit of absentmindedness. Here, evidently, she was suggesting her identity with the mythical Sita. Indeed, she may have considered herself to be a forsaken wife like Sita herself and we do know that some visitors to Dakshineswar had involuntarily made an identical suggestion, when reacting to the pitiable living conditions at the *nahabatkhana*. At times, Sarada Devi also fancied herself as the goddess Laxmi, forced to temporarily abandon her permanent residence at Vaikuntha, the heavenly abode of her husband, Lord Vishnu. She once told a devotee that but for the earthly *lila* that she was destined to play, her rightful place would have been just next to Lord Narayana. Finally, it is important not to dismiss claims often made by devotees that she had privately revealed herself before them either as the Goddess Kali or else, Jagaddhatri. However irrational or bizarre these may otherwise sound, these were perceptions that some devotees truly believed in. The list of those claiming to have had visions of her as the goddess Kali, is relatively longer. This is somewhat natural, given Sarada's close associations with her Kali-worshipping husband and the time spent at Dakshineswar. It is not fortuitous that the brigand who first had visions of her as Kali was himself a Kali worshipper as Bengal dacoits were commonly known to be.[5] Interestingly, however, Sarada Devi herself

5 In the absence of recorded details, it is impossible to tell how far the Bagdi robber's visions of the goddess Kali differed from that of Sarada's bhadralok admirers, but they must have differed in some important respects. For robbers and brigands, Kali was the source of bodily strength, power and courage and not metaphysical speculation. It is not surprising that the goddess at Dakshineswar was given the name Bhavatarini, one who freed people of their earthly share of troubles and sins. This version of Kali worship also routinely included animal sacrifice. Sarada Devi banned animal sacrifice at Belur at the behest of Mahendranath Gupta and available records would suggest that she consumed flesh of an animal sacrificed to the goddess only once, immediately following the Shodashi Puja.

questioned these ascriptions with a whiff of subtle humour. A devotee who once prepared to stab himself in her presence, ostensibly to earn some religious merit, she reprimanded quite severely. 'Have you taken me for Goddess Kali?' She had asked in a stern and disapproving voice. At another instance, a devotee told her that since he was convinced of her divine identity with Kali, she need not reveal herself in that form any more. 'What a relief!' Sarada Devi jocularly replied, 'This would mean that I no longer need to keep my tongue protruding all the time!'

In Sil's perception, the status of Holy Mother conferred on Sarada Devi was but a theological expression of an idealized cultural construct. For him, such ascriptions specially applied to the Hindu culture of ethnic Bengal with its historical grounding in Saktaism and Tantra. Prima facie this does appear to be a plausible argument. By the 1880s, eclectic Brahmos like Keshabchandra Sen too had admitted the 'motherhood of God', no doubt with some support from the teachings of Sri Ramakrishna. Tantra valourized the Feminine in more ways than one; one particular way in which it especially upheld the religious sanctity of the mother was by suggesting that she was indeed the ideal guru to initiate and train a person in spiritual life. It thus becomes tempting to forge connections between Sarada Devi's frequently initiating men and women of all ages and the 'motherhood' status attached to her. On the other hand, such connections may not be as straightforward or unproblematic as they prima facie appear. Older Sakta-Tantric literature, as typically found in the poetic compositions and songs of Ramprosad Sen (c. 18 century), at times also complain of the impermanence of earthly relations, the inscrutable ways of the Mother Goddess, but most tellingly, of the insincerity of feelings and the impatience in the human mother whose grief even at the untimely loss of a son, was cut short by her routine involvement in worldly life. Sakta poetry, more than the Vaishnava, brought out the transitory nature of the world and the elusive quality about all human relationships. Such characteristic qualities attached to the Goddess and to Sakta worship more generally make reading the life of Holy Mother along these lines somewhat difficult. Sarada Devi was anything but the capricious mother that the inscrutable Goddess herself might occasionally prove to be, and presumably, in relating to her, devotees were likely to go by her human face that was more tangible and accessible than the divine. Also interesting is the fact that in initiating men and women she often went by an intuitive understanding of their inner character and the nature of their spiritual requirements rather than established conventions. She is known to have used both Vaishnava and Sakta mantras to initiate people, which makes her anything but narrowly sectarian. Contrary to all conventions too, she would initiate a man in Vaishnava mantra even when his forbears were known to be orthodox Saktas and used Sakta mantra for a person of known Vaishnava antecedents. She generally desisted from re-initiating a devotee who already had been initiated by a *kulaguru* (hereditary gurus attached to families), but made exceptions when the devotee insisted on being initiated by her. This was more a matter of human assessment than conforming to traditions and the assessment hinged on what in particular the devotees saw in the human Saradamani. What worked here the most was possibly the warmth and kindness that one human being came to expect in another, outside social and ritual proprieties. However, this is not to suggest that the human face obliterated the divine. There is a complex interplay of the two that is at work here.

While it is entirely possible that certain established ideas or practices distinctive to Hindu-Bengali culture affirmed Sarada Devi's status as an extraordinary religious figure, we cannot lose sight of some other forces at work. There is indeed a case for arguing that certain religious ideas associated with the Ramakrishna cult only reinforced the penchant for ascribing divinity to Sarada Devi and seeking refuge in a mother-figure. This was a case of certain religious postulates further fertilizing a culture that was already weighed in favour of the mother cult. Mahendranath Gupta's *Sri Sri Ramakrishna Kathamrita* reveals that in Ramakrishna's perception, the metaphysical postulates of Brahman and Sakti/Maya were inseparable, not polarities. In this view, Sakti represented the *saguna* form of Brahman and the Brahman itself, the *nirguna* form. This places the discourse of Ramakrishna more within the Vedantic philosophical tradition than the Samkhya. Gupta himself is reported to have admitted before Swami Nityatmananda, author of *Sri Ma Darshan* (1960–76) that he took Ramakrishna and his spouse to be both born of Adyasakti (Primeval Power). This perception is endorsed by statements attributed to both Ramakrishna and Sarada Devi. We know that upon her husband's death, Sarada Devi gave out an anguished cry about Goddess Kali having unjustly forsaken her. But that apart, Ramakrishna also described himself and his wife as *sakhi*s or female companions to Kali at Dakshineswar. Sarada Devi once told a devotee that her husband had come to view every form of life in the world as emanations of the Mother and counted on her to demonstrate this Truth. Not surprisingly, hagiographic readings of Sarada have chosen to argue that while the wives of other avatars such as Sita or Vishnupriya had only served to carry forward the spiritual ideals created by their husbands, the Holy Mother alone could claim to have been a true *lilasangini*, the spouse who actively co-participated in the unfolding of some Divine play on earth initiated by the avatar, Sri Ramakrishna. This appears to have been one way in which the Ramakrishna cult and that around Saradamani intertwined, bringing the human face and the divine closer to one another.

In their own ways, some of the Western devotees of Sarada too have attached a palpable religious aura to her person. Nivedita, for instance, was happy to note that the Holy Mother preferred to remain veiled much in the manner of female Christian saints, that she liked Easter music and was impressed by the

Christian marriage vow. Sarah Bull, writing to Max Muller on 11 July 1898, insisted that Ramakrishna's widow had taken the (Christian) vows of poverty and chastity and that in willfully renouncing the natural joys of a mother, she, along with her husband, had become the spiritual parents of numerous children. This was an aspect that did not escape the attention of Eric Hammond, a disciple of Vivekananda, writing in *The Theosophical Review* of 1902. Hammond believed that Sarada Devi deserved to be placed on the pedestal of worship 'primarily because she was the widow and disciple of Ramakrishna'. I am inclined to think that even this does not really take away from the very human touch that she personally brought to bear when dealing with people. It is only apt to end here with a short extract from Betty Leggett (1852–1931) describing to Josephine McLeod (1858–1949), her sister and a disciple of Vivekananda, her meeting with the Holy Mother sometime in 1915:

> ...she talked and made many gestures of adoration and little prayer during her stories... she took my face in her hands several times and I kissed her hands, and parted several

> times with much emotion.... I...thought of the similar simplicity and almost poverty of our Madonna, who must have been so like (her) at fifty.... I had tears, and I thought she had, but I couldn't quite see for my own.[6]

The power of the human touch cannot be overlooked here nor the allusion to the Madonna.

Swami Prabhavananda later quoted Josephine McLeod as expressing herself in the following words:

'I never saw anything in her except that she was a very simple woman.'[7]

But then, Josephine was also one of those to instill in figures like Nivedita the idea that Saradamani was no ordinary human being.

6 Cited in: Gopal Stavig, *Western Admirers of Ramakrishna and His Disciples*, ed. Swami Shuddhidananda (Kolkata: Advaita Ashram, 2010), p. 211.

7 Ibid. p. 205.

SARADA DEVI:
A REAPPRAISAL

Sarada Devi survived her better-known husband by about thirty-six years. By the time she passed away in 1920, about half of Sri Ramakrishna's direct disciples were dead and gone too. But the movement and the organization launched in his name survived and gradually spread its wings to far corners of the world and for this, Sarada Devi must justly be allowed to lay some claim. What she did to advance the Ramakrishna cult is in some ways discernibly different from what the monks and lay followers performed. She was not the apologist who built an intellectual base for the movement, the crusader who actively recruited workers for the cause or even the proselyte who carried the Master's message to distant lands. She was never formally trained in the Hindu spiritual discourse or even an active practitioner of it and while some devotees and disciples did come to feel that her underlying divine qualities were but only thinly concealed behind the worldly, she ultimately comes through as an individual who never detached herself from mundane matters or shied away from the difficult choices or predicaments that once faced in everyday life. Even as she herself claimed identity with the Divine at times, it was always her attempt to humanly resolve recurring problems confronting the common man and woman. She could sympathize with the poor since she had herself known grinding poverty or could swiftly descend to the roots of some problems also because she would have the practical experience of coping with similar situations. On certain matters, she could indeed be naïve, but this was more than compensated by an engaging simplicity and frankness which managed to win hearts and instill hope and optimism even in those deeply affected by failures, cynicism or despondency. Rather than subscribing to the somewhat reductionist view that in the absence of her husband she was manipulatively catapulted to the position of a cult leader, it would be more convincing to say that this followed more from a combination of natural charisma and some compelling historical circumstances in which she was placed. Here, it would be important to remember that in Ramakrishna's lifetime, she was little known, and for a long time, the Ramakrishna Order made no particular effort to publicize her. Even as late as 1917, there were no photographs of her commonly in circulation, neither a standard biography available. The Bengali language press did not celebrate her as promptly as they had once celebrated Sri Ramakrishna. For a time, monks and lay followers did not turn out to be the active protagonists that they might have been; on the contrary, there was a transparent attempt to keep her away from public gaze; the instance to cite here typically is that of Swami Saradananda cautioning an enthusiastic would-be biographer, Labanya Kumar Chakrabarti, not to publish the work lest she be misunderstood by common men and women. It is difficult to determine just what these incipient fears were. Perhaps they related to certain unusual acts or decisions associated with Sarada Devi, as for instance, her refusal to fully adopt the dress codes of an upper-caste Hindu widow or freely socializing with non-Hindus or even the fact that her claims to holiness could not be supported by references to any demonstrated praxis and recognition by contemporary sadhus or saints. In the case of Ramakrishna, public acknowledgement would have at least partly arisen in holy men repeatedly calling on him at Dakshineswar and Ramakrishna's own visits to several religious fairs and congregations in and around Calcutta. Sarada Devi's devotees may indeed have feared that some acts of Sarada could be quite easily misunderstood and even socially resisted. For the common people not to view these as departures from convention, a new social and spiritual rationale had to be put in place. The rationale had to be built upon new projections of charisma and invested with new meanings. Especially after 1891, the two faces of Sarada Devi, the human and the divine had to be more closely integrated. By itself, neither of these would have worked as powerfully. The status of 'Sanghajanani', though functionally created by the Ramakrishna monks for their own purposes, could be amplified through a growing public participation in the process of hagiographical celebration.

Prima facie, to frame a connected and coherent analysis of the life and work of Sarada Devi is no easy task. For one, on most issues, she exhibited startling contradictions and paradoxes as did her husband. On the whole though, she was on the side of respecting conventional ways of life and never adopted a radically rebellious approach. And yet, she did not always passively accept socially entrenched ideas or practices and found ways in which to assert her private judgment or opinion. On certain matters she could be forthright and stubborn and refused to be cowed down by social pressure. On the issue of man-woman relationships, she was no means a feminist and yet even in a world ruled by patriarchy, found space to express forms of disapproval or dissent. She did not actively implicate herself in agendas that contemporary reformist bodies had adopted for themselves, as for instance, promoting female education, widow marriages or prohibiting polygamy; on the other hand, she revealed an acute empathy and understanding of the social injustices and insensitivity that women in particular were continually subjected to. She was positively angry when told that pregnant woman had been made to march barefoot to the local police station for interrogation and wailed uncontrollably upon hearing of mothers labouring hard at work sites to supplement their meagre family incomes, being forced to leave their newborn babies unattended for several hours at a stretch. Such reactions emanated not in Sarada Devi's playing out some apocryphal or supra-natural roles, but in spontaneous feelings exhibited by someone deeply sensitized to the vagaries of human existence.

Unlike Sri Ramakrishna, Sarada Devi did not consider the life of a householder to be an impediment to spiritual life and her understanding of just how men and women ought to conduct themselves in the world reveals significant overlaps with what her husband generally recommended to his devotees and disciples. For one, Sri Ramakrishna himself tutored Sarada in the virtues of feminine restraint, patience and modesty. He even expressed some anxiety with regard to the sexual safety of his wife in male company and here he made no exceptions with even close male relatives. For instance, he was unhappy at his nephews Ramlal and Hriday spending long hours at the *nahabat*, chatting in the company of their aunt and he specifically warned Sarada herself never to accept anyone's hospitality lest people feel encouraged to make scandalous advances. Ramakrishna did not encourage his wife to cultivate ecstatic moods (*bhava*) for fear that this would make her unmindful of propitious conduct on the part of a woman in public. On this question, he felt, any comparisons drawn between his wife and Gauri Ma were flawed since the latter was 'a woman from Kalighat' who had come to see the world differently.[1] Sarada Devi herself discouraged women dancing freely to the tune of Vaishnava devotional singing (kirtanas) since such acts, allegedly, became the focus of illicit male attention.

Before she moved into her permanent home at Bagbazar, Sarada Devi, whenever in Calcutta, would often reside with the families of either Balaram Basu or else Mahendranath Gupta, two of the closest devotees of Sri Ramakrishna. In some ways, her conservatism went beyond that of Ramakrishna himself. Unlike her husband, she did not think that in the pursuit of spiritual life, a woman could ever lose sight of rules of decorum and modesty. That liberty only a man could safely take. Interestingly enough, she did not also think that women were truly capable of intense spells of yogic meditation (*dhyan*) and that in their case, the routine chanting of the beads and mantra (*japa*) would suffice. But there was also a liberal side to her which, at times, was quite palpable. For instance, she did not think marriage was incumbent upon all girls and to mothers who found it difficult to get their daughters married by a certain age,

1 Swami Gambhirananda, in explaining this remark made by Ramakrishna, tells us that since Gauri Ma was from a priestly family, she was more accustomed to public gaze and had grown to be an extrovert.

her advice was to get them educated. Her nieces, Radhu and Nalini, received primary education in a school run by Christian missionaries, a choice that would have ordinarily deterred parents of even boys. After 1898, she had Sister Nivedita's Girls' school in Bagbazar to recommend. She took personal interest in the school and occasionally met students at work and play. She had high praise for her spiritual companion, Gauri Ma, who also started a training school and ashram and even managed to procure a horse-drawn carriage for transporting girl students. In Sarada Devi's perception, Gauri Ma's energy and enterprise made her more a man than a woman. The Saradeswari Ashram itself, that Gauri Ma ran, lived up to certain ideals inspired by the Holy Mother. For one, the name Saradeswari could have been inspired by Sarada Devi herself but more interestingly, inmates of the Ashram were made to wear a red-bordered sari even though they were training to be female ascetics. They were ritually married to Lord Narayan (Vishnu) so as to secure their connection with a husband who was not commonplace but immortal. In the years to follow, Nivedita's school, which still survives as Ramakrishna Sarada Mission Girls' School, performed admirably. With substantial help from the American social worker, Christine Greenstidel (1866–

1930) and Sudhira Basu (Sister Sudhira, 1889–1920), this school became the nucleus of a movement that promoted self-help among young girls. They were taught various craft-skills and marketing their products even fetched them modest incomes.

Admittedly, Sarada Devi was not always an unquestioning supporter of social conventions and at times articulated signs of feminine empowerment and courageous resistance. To a fisherwoman of Jairambati who had been ill treated by her husband she advised:

> Do not go out of your way to please your husband through sweet talk. Carry out all your household work dutifully and see to it that you attend to all your husband's needs. But do make sure that you show no eagerness to make it up with him. It is important that he too be made to understand that your place in his everyday life is no less important.

However, such bold expressions have sometimes been taken out of their context and misinterpreted. It has been argued for instance, that her personally refusing to take off her gold bangles or wearing a red-bordered sari was tantamount to rejecting the institution of widowhood itself. In hindsight, this would be hard to defend if only because she followed the orthodox rules governing Hindu widowhood in almost every other aspect. Her approach, more often than not, was a mix of careful conventionalism and judicious realism. She saw nothing wrong in child widows being allowed to consume fish, contrary to custom, but also expected them to fall in with socially accepted conventions by the time they had turned into adults. It was cruel of the community to impose harsh dietary regimes on young girls who could barely understand the social meaning behind such self-restraint and taboos, she argued. The community's denying them such small pleasures they would interpret as unnaturally stifling for their body and soul. This was a grievance that young girls ought not to nurse growing into adulthood, she felt, for it both damaged the moral fibre of the society and encouraged wanton rebelliousness. Our sources reveal that Sarada Devi otherwise showed the same concern that bhadralok society generally showed towards the sexual vulnerability of the unprotected Hindu widow. 'Move about with the utmost caution,' she would advise young widows, 'Don't even look at a man, far less trust him.' And here, Sarada's advice on the perils of unbridled sexuality parallels that offered by her husband, albeit from the opposite end:

> My child, do not ever trust a man. With a man you cannot really set apart one who can be trusted from one that cannot be. Do not trust your father, your brothers or even God Himself should he appear before you in the guise of a man!

She reprimanded married women visitors who displayed no vermillion mark on their person and was positively peeved by the anxious wife who, even when soliciting her blessings for an ailing husband, appeared before her bedecked in fine clothes, jewellery and with liberal doses of perfume applied to her person. Feminine beauty was short-lived, she maintained, and women who boasted of their beauty might be taken to have seriously gone astray. She once defended Radhu's husband, Manmathnath Chattopadhyay, for slapping his wife after she had angrily thrown a towel at him, admonished Radhu herself for indecorously lifting her sari above her knees, Nalini for chanting mantras in public view when bathing in the Ganges and advised a woman to amicably patch up her differences with a co-wife for the sake of the harried husband's peace of mind. The *Kathamrita* records Ramakrishna's disenchantment at women who even after repeatedly suffering the trauma of child birth would still not desist from uniting with her husband. Sarada Devi's counsel to niece Maku (Sushila) replicates this exactly:

> Happiness in conjugal life is as fragile and short-lived as the happiness that one may expect to experience in this world. Have you no shame in repeatedly joining your husband in bed? Why this animal attraction?...Can you not live as brothers and sisters?

Sarada Devi generally upheld the idea that a woman had to be put under the care of a man at every important stage of her life, under the father when a child and the husband when married. Her social conservatism could occasionally extend to other matters. She disapproved of a devotee, who had travelled to the West, marrying an English woman and another male devotee, who was Brahmin by birth, marrying a woman belonging to the marginalized Mahisya caste. Reportedly, both male devotees gave in to her wishes.

The interesting thing though is that such conservatism has to be read together with startling exceptions she made with regard to taboos of ritual purity and pollution. Sushilabala Dutta, a Barujibi by caste (traditionally agriculturalists and betel leaf growers), was permitted to cook for her and Sarada Devi was unruffled by the resentment expressed at Sister Nivedita being once permitted to cook and serve food to Ramakrishna as part of the daily services at Bagbazar. She severely chastised Nalini on refusing to serve food in a proper manner to Amjad, a Muslim devotee, for fear of ritual contamination. Bhaktas had no caste, they were a caste by themselves—Sarada Devi was heard to say, much in the manner of Ramakrishna himself. Another time, when uncle Nilmadhav died, one of the people carrying the dead body to the cremation ground happened to be a non-Brahmin. When Nalini objected to a Shudra's being allowed to carry a Brahmin's body, Sarada Devi sharply interjected, 'Who is a Shudra, Nalini?' she asked, with some pain in her voice. Showing affection, care and grace to a devotee, regardless of operative social and ritual conventions especially pleased Sarada, and here, one may detect a subtle overlapping of tender motherliness for a child in need and a spontaneous concern and respect for the well being of a devotee. She volunteered to wash Girishchandra's bed roll, even though the man was by birth a Kayastha. On another occasion, she personally washed the bed of a female guest at Jairambati, who had been suffering from malarial fever and involuntarily soiled the bed one night. Allowing for exceptions, she showed exemplary courage and fortitude in setting aside certain established norms that surprised her devotees, both Indian and Western. Sometimes, though, she was unable to resist or overlook the power of everyday social conventions and significantly enough, this occurred both at Jairambati and Calcutta. In her native village, Sarada Devi ran into serious trouble when Brahman guests invited to a meal refused to be served by Brahmacharis of the Ramakrishna Order on the ground that their castes were unknown. Whenever Sister Devmata (Laura Glenn) called on Sarada at the Bagbazar residence, she was welcomed, but once she left, the spot where she was seated had to be ritually purified with a sprinkling of cow dung water.

Certain inner conflicts pervaded the spiritual life of Sarada Devi. In hindsight, it would be reasonable to note the two very different perceptions that Sarada Devi exhibited in her role as a spiritual guide and counsellor. By one estimate, she could grant *mantra disksha* up to thirty to thirty-five people in a single day and this was a task that she generally carried out ungrudgingly. Among the direct disciples of Sri Ramakrishna, she is known to have initiated were Trigunatitananda, Yogananda and going by one version, Abhedananda as well.[2] She is also known to have offered the ochre robe of the sanyasi (*gerua*) directly to at least three disciples including Jitendranath Ray (Swami Vishudhananda, 1883–1962, the eighth president of the Ramakrishna Mission). She was the spiritual preceptor to Kalikrishna Bose (Swami Virajanada, 1873–1951), Sushil Chandra Chakrabarty (Swami Prakashananda, 1974–1927, associated with the Vedanta Society of San Francisco) and Dineshchandra Das Gupta (Swami Nikhilananda, 1893–1973), the founder of the Ramakrishna Vedanta Centre of New York in 1933.[3] Barring rare exceptions, she appears to have patiently put up with the unreasonable demands made on her by impatient and impulsive devotees,

2 Sarada Devi's first biographer, Brahmachari Akshaychaitanya, makes this claim.

3 In his early life, Swami Nikhilananda was a political worker who was released from police custody in 1918.

unmindful of what discomfort or distress this might bring to the Holy Mother herself. A young devotee by the name of Satyendranath Majumdar once found middle class male devotees sobbing loudly before the Mother when narrating their woes, not pausing to think about the long queue of visitors that was building up behind them. Others subjected her to the acute discomfort of remaining fixed in a certain pose, fully wrapped in coarse cloth even on a hot summer day in Calcutta. Still others would not have the patience to wait their turn and left in a hurry, wildly flinging away their rosary. Upon getting back home, they wrote abusive letters addressed to Sarada Devi. Majumdar, who was quite peeved at such proceedings, once asked Sarada why she agreed to withstand such ordeals, upon which the Holy Mother graciously told him how he was too young to fathom the existential trauma and troubles that people were habitually compelled to face. And yet, there is some evidence to show that she also harboured an inner resentment at putting up with such demanding routines. On one level, she appears to have been resentful of the way she had been increasingly exposed to public gaze and made to routinely carry out spiritual services, even at the cost of causing her some irritation and discomfort.

For this, however, she blamed Mahendranath Gupta the most for having so widely publicized the Ramakrishna cult. Here, it would be important to recall that the author of the *Kathamrita* himself sought words of support and encouragement from the Holy Mother to authenticate himself and his reporting.[4] 'Thakur (Ramakrishna) always ensured that I was hidden from public view, handling me with due discretion and care,' she once grudgingly told a devotee, 'Now, they (his devotees) are publicizing me with the loud beating of drums at the market place!'

While kindness and compassion, as she herself claimed, persuaded her to initiate seekers, she also viewed this act as causing her mental trauma and physical pain. At the Durga Puja festivities of 1916 at Belur, which she personally attended, a huge gathering of people thronged to see her, bowing down to touch her feet and seeking her blessings, as was common custom. Reportedly, Sarada Devi reacted to this with some sense of consternation. Here is what she told a devotee present at the spot:

4 The Kathamrita Bhavan edition of the *Sri Sri Ramkrishna Kathamrita* carries a letter of recommendation from the Holy Mother stating that what Gupta reported were indeed the words uttered by Ramakrishna himself.

> Oh do keep fanning me, my child! My whole body is virtually on fire! Enough of the people of Calcutta! Some come and complain before me of one form of suffering they were going through, others of another kind. This is not something that I can patiently endure. Some, having led a bad life in the past, are now too eager to recant; others unthinkingly gave birth to twenty five children and keep crying their hearts out because ten of those died prematurely! These are not human beings I see before me, only beasts. They have no sense of discrimination and nothing resembling self-restraint. My child, I can no longer bear to see such sorrow and suffering!

The Holy Mother repeatedly asserted that people touching her feet by way of seeking blessings transferred the cumulative weight of their sins on to her, causing a burning sensation in her feet. In such instances, she would instruct some of her devotees to keep pouring water on her feet, so as to take away some of this sensation. Again, this has much in common with the experiences of Ramakrishna who would similarly worry about the guru having to take on the burden of the sins of his disciples. What is interesting here too is Sarada Devi's tacit unhappiness at the fact that people chose to come to her for initiation, rather than seek out the monks at Belur. On occasions, she wondered if Ramakrishna had conspired to have the best of disciples to himself, leaving the human rubble to her! What also worried and turned her unhappy is the way some people insisted on seeking initiation under her notwithstanding the fact that they already had a family guru (*kulaguru*). She would have been aware as any other that this was clearly a violation of established traditions. Multiple religious tutors (*sikshaguru*) were permitted but never multiple spiritual preceptors (*dikshaguru*). At times, she did also grudgingly give vent to the view that as much as she would have liked, she still could not redeem all seekers since upon attempting to do so, her own powers would be seriously diluted. The irony here though is that she also said things completely to the contrary. Having complained of the discomfort or pain that people allegedly subjected her to, she has also gone on record saying how if it was not for gurus like her, people would never be redeemed of their bad karma or sins. She also fully believed in the power and potentiality of her spiritual initiation. Those who had been so initiated would not be subjected to rebirth, she is known to have prophesized.

Another feature that Sarada Devi had in common with her husband, Sri Ramakrishna, was the delicate balance of approach when it came to comparing monks to lay devotees. One of the enduringly attractive teachings of Ramakrishna pertains to his likening the householder's life to the fortress from within which the hardest moral and spiritual battles could be successfully waged. Renunciation was indeed important, but it did not suit all. Also, it was actually more a matter of renouncing—not the world itself but worldliness. Sri Ramakrishna told Mahendranath Gupta that it would suffice to periodically rupture the routines of everyday life by temporarily retreating to the solitude of spiritual praxis (*sadhana*). And yet, both Ramakrishna and Sarada undoubtedly valourized the life of the monastic, however ambiguously. Sarada Devi's advice to monks of the Ramakrishna Order was never to depend on the patronage of the *grihastha* (householder). In return for a small act of charity, they might stoop to the level of getting a monk to carry their baggage, she warned a young monk, who was hoping to obtain to travel gratis in the company of householder devotees. However, the life of the monk was hard and weighed down with rigorous self-discipline. A monk could not so much as cast a glance at a woman, for apart from the pitfalls of an acquisitive spirit and the lure of material wealth (*kanchan*), what most effectively took away from a man's spiritual life was sexual attraction for the lascivious female (*kamini*). It was far better to enter a marital life, Sarada Devi argued, than to lead the life of the *neda-nedis*[5] who unscrupulously adopted a life of free gender mixing. Sarada herself would not permit female ascetics adorning the *gerua* to reverentially touch her feet.[6] At Jairambati, she preferred to feed monks alone small quantities of milk that she could occasionally obtain from her neighbours. Householders had greater access to such indulgences, she ruled; who cared for the sanyasi? What irked her though, to cite yet another instance of the complexities involved here, was the news of monks arrogating to themselves a position far superior to that of the householders. She was positively upset upon

5 The expression literally means the shaven headed and traditionally referred to members of an allegedly 'degenerate' Buddhism and popular Vaishnava cults who flouted many social rules originating in Brahamanism.

6 Reportedly, Ramakrishna himself forbade Sarada to put on the ochre robe that had been presented to her by the wife of the philanthropist, Jadu Mallik.

hearing how at the Belur Math, pillows ordinarily meant for monks but inadvertently used by a householder devotee had to be simply thrown away.

There is one matter on which Sarada Devi significantly differed from the position adopted by her husband, Sri Ramakrishna. This was with regard to the question of whether or not socially and ethically responsible work affected advancement in spiritual life. This controversy followed from older perceptions about work only adding to material embroilment and worldliness. In classical Vedantic thought, all transformations resulting from activity belonged to the domain of Maya or the Great Illusion. Brahman (Absolute/God) was absolute precisely on account of its inert and immutable character. Sri Ramakrishna was disappointed to hear that some of his philanthropic minded devotees planned to expend their energies and resources upon building charitable hospitals and dispensaries. Man's primary purpose in life, as he saw it, was God-realization and anything that distracted from that had to be avoided. Sarada Devi on the other hand, proved to be pragmatic and more sensitized to contemporary conditions. 'Thakur' (Ramakrishna) had his generous patrons who met all his recurring everyday needs but such good fortune would not come to all monks or renouncers. Monks would simply languish and starve if they did not occupy themselves in some form of activity or the other and besides, work had its own instructive value. In 1912, when visiting the Kashi Sevashram, an institution run by local monks belonging to the Ramakrishna Order, she donated a sum of Rs 10 towards social service and encouraged them to extend the idea of *seva* or selfless service to the people in need.

Sarada Devi did not develop a coherent body of religious thought and barring a few exceptions, much of what she articulated only reaffirmed the teachings of Sri Ramakrishna. For one, she did not think that religion was a matter of disputation; such propensities only reflected the vacuous pedantry of the Gnostics (*jnani*). To this she added that women were even less likely to realize God by employing the intellect. Pious devotion and simply the love of God was a far easier and effective method of realizing God. This calls to mind Sri Ramakrishna's characterizing bhakti itself as typically feminine and pointing to the very futility of frivolous debates around God and religion. Disputations only fanned the gratuitous human ego and a man's sense of authority and agency (*kartitwa*) whereas in truth, that very ego and agency had to give way to a loving surrender before God. And what did happen after all, once a man realized God, she quizzed; did he suddenly grow a pair of horns? In Sarada Devi's view, religious experience only brought forth powers of discrimination (*bairagya*), enabling us to realize the transitory nature of the world itself and human life within it. In a manner befitting, the Vedantin held that wisdom only brought us palpably closer to admitting the Transcendental and to the realization that multiple gods or deities simply belonged to the domain of beguiling Maya. These were simply human conceptions that temporarily appeared in time and also disappeared with it.

There were two very interesting and original statements about Sri Ramakrishna himself that the Holy Mother is known to have made. In the first place, she ranked him as a supreme conversationalist even to the point of being garrulous and a man who could effectively mask the most sombre thoughts in candid merriment. 'He was *anandamay* (full of joyous bliss), I have never seen the man go morose or unhappy,' she once quipped.

The other observation she made is as original as it is interesting:

> Everyone claims that he (Ramakrishna) preached the harmony of religions. But know this: the various religious traditions that he experimented with were not aimed at accomplishing this harmony. His sole purpose was simply to determine how the same God could be invoked in different religious languages and through various means.

This has an uncanny resemblance to the observation once made by the orientalist, Nathaniel Brassey Halhed (1751–1830). In his *A Code of Gentoo Laws or Ordinations of the Pundits* (1775), Halhed made a note of 'that article of faith among Brahmins that God's all merciful power would not have permitted such a number of different religions if He had not also found pleasure of beholding their varieties.'[7]

Prima facie, Ramakrishna's ecumenical approach to religions was at times overridden by certain notions of cultural insularity. The *Kathamrita* clearly reveals his

7 This also encourages us to look more critically at claims being made to this day about Ramakrishna 'harmonizing' various religions. For a recent work highlighting the 'harmonization', see Ayon Maharaj, Infinite Paths to *Infinite Reality: Ramakrishna and Cross Cultural Philosophy of Religions* (New Delhi: Oxford University Press, South Asia Edition, 2019).

disapproval of both 'new-fangled' reformist religions like Brahmoism and non-conformist popular religious cults associated with Bauls and Sahajiyas. In his opinion, Sanatan Dharma (meaning orthodox Brahmanical religion) would outrun and outlive them all. Whereas Sri Ramakrishna was positively disenchanted to hear of the poet Madhusudan Dutta's (1824–73) converting to Christianity, Sarada Devi took quite gracefully to the presence of Europeans, expressed an interest in Easter music and in the Christian marriage vow and eagerly comforted a European lady who had come to seek her blessings for an ailing daughter. The Ramakrishna Order made much of the fact that in 1910, when visiting the Kothar Ashram (in Odissa) she helped to reclaim for Hinduism, the local postmaster, a Brahmin by the name of Debendranath Chattopadhyay who had converted to Christianity. Chattopadhyay was later reinvested with the sacred thread by one of the monks present on the occasion; by comparison, Sarada Devi herself had practically nothing to say of the episode.

In 1953, on the occasion of the centenary celebrations of Sarada Devi, her first biographer Brahmachari Akshaychaitanya published a list of 1,176 men and women who had been granted *mantra diksha* by the Holy Mother.[8] The list, as the Brahmachari claims, was painstakingly compiled over several years, well into the riot-affected years of 1946–47. An analysis of the information so provided proved interesting. Of the 1,176 so initiated, about 600 were personally known to Akshaychaitanya. This is indicative both of the genuineness of the list and of the numbers involved. The list covers 11 districts of present-day Bangladesh (Chittagong, Noakhali, Sylhet, Dhaka, Mymensing, Faridpur, Bakargunj, Pabna Khulna, Jessore and Rajshahi), 14 districts and towns in Bengal, Tripura and Assam (Cachar, Cooch Behar, Dinajpur, Malda, Nadia, Murshidabad, 24 Paraganas, Hoogly, Calcutta, Howrah, Bankura, Burdwan, Birbhum and Manbhum), 3 districts in Orissa (Balasore, Cuttack and Puri), 3 towns and cities of UP (Benares, Allahabad and Almora), Bombay and the southern states of Kerala and Karnataka. The USA is included in the list, but without the state or city being mentioned in every case. Predictably, the highest concentration of those initiated occurs in the city of

8 The list has been reprinted as *Sri Sri Mayer Mantrashishya Parichay* and appended to Swami Purnatmananda compiled and edited; see *Sri Sri Mayer Padaprante*, Vol. 2 (Kolkata: Udbodhan), pp. 443–485. Any statistical analysis of the people listed here could be misleading since towns like Allahabad, Benares or Calcutta are listed alongside districts.

Calcutta followed closely by Dhaka and Mymensing. Only an insignificant proportion of those so initiated went on to formally accept *sanyas*. Somewhat surprisingly, the proportion of monks to lay devotees is the highest in Sylhet[9] (18 of the 58) and Faridpur (16 of the 69). Only 14 of those 159 initiated in Calcutta[10] took to a monastic life. On a rough count, 294 of the 1,176 people initiated were women (married and unmarried). The proportion of women to the total number initiated was the highest in Calcutta; where 79 of the 159 listed here are women.

Sarada Devi is known to have initiated (in 1911) at least one European male of Dutch origin, Cornelis Johannes Heijblom (later Swami Atulananda, 1870–1966), who been had earlier drawn to the Vedanta through influences cast by Swamis Vivekananda and Abhedananda.[11]

9 Brahmachari Akshaychaitanya himself was from Sylhet. Also from Sylhet was Mira Devi who formally accepted *sanyas* and joined the Sarada Ashram.

10 The list for Calcutta includes swamis Abhedananda and Trigunatitananda, Virjananda and Yogananda. Also included are Durgapuri Devi who was associated with the Saradeswari Ashram, Parul Mukhopadhyay (later Pravrajika Bharatiprana, head of the Sarada Math) and the well-known women author -activists, Saralabala Sarkar (1857–1961) and her daughter Nirjharini Sarkar (1894–1963).

11 Surprisingly though, his book—*With the Swamis in America* (1938)—mentions very little of his meeting with Sarada Devi or days in Calcutta.

One other interesting and important difference between Sri Ramakrishna and Sarada Devi hinges on their social constituency. Early biographies and sundry articles appearing in journals pertaining to Ramakrishna originated in broadly two kinds of sources: his middle class followers (monks and laymen) based in India and Western admirers whose major source of information were also Indians. Max Muller, who never personally visited India, based his writings on Ramakrishna almost entirely on the information provided by swamis Vivekananda and Saradananda. In the case of Sarada Devi, there is a discernible shift of trajectory in two respects. No scholar or observer of Western origin has produced a full length biography of the Holy Mother, whether in her own time or thereafter.[12] On the other hand, the literature available on Sarada in the form of reminiscences or memoirs has a discernibly mixed class character, going by the people who have contributed to this substantial body of literature. For Sarada, there is a surprisingly large number of anecdotes and rambling reminiscences originating in people of a relatively non-

12 A work originally written in French by Solange LeMaitre (*Ramakrishna el le Vitalite de Hindouism*) and dating back to 1959 mentions her tangentially and in a strongly hagiographic vein. The English version called *Sri Ramakrishna and the Vitality of Hinduism* appeared in 1984.

descript character: manual labourers, farmers, fishermen and fisherwoman, palki-bearers, part-time domestic workers, scavengers and even such characters who may have intermittently taken to brigandage. Importantly, a good number of these accounts carry the name of the author which would suggest that they were somewhat anxious to provide a personal touch to their narratives. We thus hear of the Muslim neighbour Amjad, his wife, Malijan Bibi, and his mother, Fatima, who often turned up at Sarada Devi's residence and were fed on puffed rice and molasses. Shantiram Das, a palki-bearer by profession who carried her to Vishnupur on occasions testifies as to how she spoke haltingly in a sweet voice. Das also speaks of his aged mother once employed by Sarada as a domestic help continuing to sweep the courtyard at Jairambati even after her employer was dead and gone, only to bring back memories of the Mother who once walked across that courtyard. The woman of Sadgop caste, Nistarini Devi, tells us of how overawed she was upon seeing the Holy Mother unassumingly work as an ordinary village woman would, winnowing paddy, feeding the cows and diligently preparing cow dung cakes to be used as kitchen fuel. At the Vishnupur railway station, she extended her grace to Prahlad, a man of the local Lohar (blacksmith) community who said he had visions of Sita in her. In Jairambati, Basanabala, widowed at the tender age of seven, also employed by Sarada in 1882 as a domestic help, served her for as many as ten years. In Calcutta, she catered to a different class and made a personal effort to connect with them. She visited the homes of Rai Bahadur Madhav Chandra in the old Ballygunj area and Rajlaxmi Basu, wife of a District Judge. At both these places the hosts entertained her by playing kirtan songs on gramophone records which, reportedly, she very much enjoyed.[13] At the Udbodhan residence a certain Brahmo lady doctor by the name of Dr Pramada Dutta, happily agreed to accept prasad from her hands, shaking off all her inhibitions. She met such devotees or admirers and many others with an air of disarming simplicity and grace, and also comforted them with reassuring words. To Chapalasundari Dasi,[14]

13 Both Gauri Ma and Yogin Ma have testified to Sarada Devi's fondness for songs and music. She was often invited to watch plays of Girishchandra Ghosh enacted at various theatres. Between the years 1910 and 1918 she watched the following plays by Girshchandra: *Vilwamangal, Chaitanya lila, Jana, Pandav Gaurav, Daksha Yajnya* and *Kinnari.*

14 Wife of Chandramaohan Dutta from Dhaka, Vikrampur, who was practically a fugitive in Calcutta for some time, but much to his relief offered petty employment as a book packer and vendor by the Udbodhan office and who claims to have had visions of the Holy Mother as Jagaddhatri herself.

a woman devotee from east Bengal and to Surendranath Sen, civil surgeon at Monghyr, she held out promises of never ever having to go without a square meal a day. More generally though, she reminded her guests and visitors that they could always count on falling back on the blessings and benediction of a mother figure.

Not many of those she granted initiation could call on her regularly for they came to her from distant lands and Sarada Devi's own movements between Jairambati and Calcutta remained uncertain for quite some time. It is also reasonable to suppose that some others failed to regularly carry out the spiritual regime that they had to follow initiation. In a few instances, the Holy Mother volunteered to carry out such tasks for them,[15] albeit only temporarily. This is comparable to Sri Ramakrishna's concept of a devotee granting his guru the *baklama* or the mandate to observe certain spiritual routines on his behalf. The interesting thing here though is that in many cases, men and women could relate to her simply as a matter of personal regard or faith, not necessarily to find hopes of redemption in her unassuming gestures and kind words. Swami Ishanananda who has left behind

15 Surendranath Bandopadhyay is one such case reported.

insightful reminiscences of the Holy Mother puts this rather well in the following words:

> Among her countless devotees I have also caught sight of those who did not covet for themselves a good reputation, personal fame, or even material wealth. There are also those who simply had no desire to be granted feelings of pious devotion or release from the endless (karmic) cycles of life and death or even in some miraculous occurrence. To the Holy Mother they had neither prayer to convey nor some complaint or remonstration.

There is a persuasive school of thought which would have us believe that many of Sarada's devotees manipulatively cast her in a political image representing Indian resistance to alien British rule. This syncs well with the broader argument that Hindu nationalism successfully appropriated powerful symbolisms latent in the idea of a motherhood, projecting the 'Mother' as both the begetter of heroic children and a symbol of active resistance. This was very much the intended meaning in novels like *Anandamath* (1882) of Bankimchandra

Chattopadhyay (1838–94) in which patriotic *santans* (literally children) rally around a ravaged and enslaved motherland and wage violent wars to rescue her from alien control. Visions of the motherland here are deliberately made interchangeable with those of the primeval Mother Goddess in keeping with older Sanskrit poetic traditions and hence, human efforts to rescue her transcend a mere political conflict and turn into something of a sacred mission. An unpublished thesis authored by a contemporary Canadian scholar quite purposively uses the expression 'Mother of India' to describe the mother figure tendentiously constructed around the person of Sarada Devi herself.[16] Historians cannot be unmindful of contexts and surely, it is quite possible that perceptions of the human mother and the divine are tactically conflated. And yet, contexts can sometimes be overdrawn. In recent years, the charisma and popular appeal of a person such as Sri Ramakrishna himself has been understood as essentially originating in the social and political duress generated by colonialism: the saint here remains very much a captive of bhadralok anxieties and imagination that gives expression to

16 Trishia Nicole Goulet, *The Lives of Sarada Devi: Gender, Renunciation and Politics in Colonial India* (PhD Thesis, Department of Religion, University of Manitoba, Winnipeg, 2009).

political aspirations in a culturally coded language.[17] The Canadian scholar cited above, would have us believe that Ramakrishna himself was made to represent an alternative to 'imperialist religiosity'.

It is doubtful if either Sarada Devi herself was cognizant of such an image of herself being constructed or that she encouraged this in any way. Such possibilities, as we may recall, are prima facie negated by her reckoning Englishmen as equally as her children who were Indians. Sarada Devi had little understanding of the reigning political concepts of Swadeshi and Boycott or the moral justification of the agitation that had grown around these. This is evident from her consumerist preference for foreign cloth over the home-spun variety, simply on grounds of its superior quality. However, this is not to suggest that she remained blind or insensitive to the conditions generally prevailing in the country. She had all praise for Queen Victoria, a sentiment also shared at one time by many patriotic Bengali men. On the other hand, she did come to believe that for the common people, living conditions had only worsened with time. She noticed the serious shortage of cloth during the war

17 This is discussed in: Amiya P. Sen, *Three Essays on Ramakrishna and His Times* (Shimla: IIAS, 2001).

years of 1914–18, and was especially upset upon hearing that some women, unable to procure cheap clothing for themselves, had been driven to commit suicide. To the schoolteacher Prabodh Chattopadhyay, who jubilantly claimed that British rule had visibly improved the material state of the country, she retorted by saying how, on the contrary, the country continued to suffer acute shortages of items even of everyday use. She was quite aware of how the Koalpara Ashram had become the refuge of several young political workers; in 1918, the police were indeed forced to conduct extended raids to flush out swadeshi workers. But this only made her marvel at how the words of Thakur (Ramakrishna) and Noren (Vivekananda) had made the people of the country quite 'fearless'. In these matters, some of her thoughts, one has to say, were also quite pragmatic. She encouraged one of her devotees, Harendranath Dasgupta, to accept the post of a daroga only so that he could serve his country by way of treating political detainees with greater kindness and consideration. Once, when the monks at Belur Math came under some pressure from the government to weed out political activists who had blended in with other inmates, she remained firm and ruled that her 'sons' who had chosen to live a monastic life under the inspiration of Ramakrishna, ought not to give in to such haughty demands. At least two young men, who were erstwhile members of the secret revolutionary society called Anusilan, were known to her. One of these later took to a monastic life and came to be known as Swami Abhayananda.[18]

However, some political comments attributed to her appear to be quite dubious. Upon hearing of President Wilson declaring his Fourteen Points at the end of the First World War, she is reported to have said that the political leaders of the West were insincere and never truly meant what they publicly said! It would be reasonable to argue that she lacked the political acumen to judge such events one way or another.

Swami Tapasyananda, one of the early biographers of Sarada Devi, neatly summed up her contributions to the Ramakrishna cult in what appears to be a well crafted panegyric. Her first major contribution to the movement, the swami argued, was to propagate the idea that an

18 I have not been able to find any conclusive evidence to determine if Swami Abhayananda was the monk popularly known as Bharat Maharaj. It is quite clear though that monastic names conferred on monks are not always exclusive to them. Swami Abhayananda was also the name given to the well-known archivist and historian, Marie Louise Burke, one of the earliest woman disciples to enter the Ramakrishna Order.

aspirant's spiritual potentiality was unfolded by his service to Sri Ramakrishna, by admitting that the Master was indeed a living presence. Second, that it was her life and not so much that of Ramakrishna which exemplified the idea of living in the world and yet not being enslaved by it. Third, Sarada Devi, in the swami's opinion, harmonized the functions of the wife, nun and mother, and here, he readily borrows the idea, first articulated by Sister Nivedita, that the Holy Mother represented the last word of Sri Ramakrishna on ideal womanhood. Her life, the Swami tells us, proved that wifely devotion was possible without sexual attraction and motherly love too without bearing children. To put it in the swami's own words, her life demonstrated the possibility of the 'highest godliness in the midst of common avocations'. Swami Tapasyananda, however, ends on a note of ill-concealed anxiety. He is clearly discomfited by the contemporary woman's undue aspiration to reach masculine standards. This was a process, he feared, by which the woman risked losing her soul.

Understandably, such statements have drawn reactions from feminist scholars who speak of the 'many' Saradas born of tendentious constructions on the part of devotees, lay and monastic alike. They further claim that rather than passively admitting to the dictates of a patriarchal society or to a monastic order entirely controlled by males, she managed to create her own space and to register small but significant acts of defiance. Thus, the refusal to remove her bangles is seen to take her outside of Hindu domestic religion. Her illiteracy, rather than revealing ignorance, is seen to represent a form of innocence and purity, untouched by a pretentious, urban middle class life. For feminist scholars, Sarada Devi was a guru in her own right who advanced on a path she herself chose and not simply a pale shadow or even a helpmate to her well-known husband. Arguably, the focus here shifts from Ramakrishna's introducing his wife into an austere and pure spiritual life to one where his own standing as a spiritual figure is aided and abetted by what his wife performed.

Feminist readings of Sarada Devi serve as a useful corrective to both zealously devotional readings of her life and the tendency to overlook the category of female renunciation altogether. From the traditional perspective, it was unnatural for a woman to renounce the world, since socially and culturally, she was always implicated in worldly life-renewal processes of procreation, feeding and nurturing. That was her natural dharma (*stridharma*). On the other hand, there is substantial evidence that supports the view that Hinduism has always left space for female asceticism, even when this has been known to assume complex forms. Among Sarada's own devotees and close companions were respected women saints, like Gauri Ma and Yogin Ma, who widely travelled and spent a good part of their lives in solitary ascetic practices. By comparison, Sarada Devi herself was not an ascetic and this probably brings into focus the distinction that Sri Ramakrishna was known to have made between 'external' renunciation and the 'internal'. The first of these turned the act of renunciation into an institution, uprooting one from the ties and functions of everyday social life; the second permitted, and no less effectively, practising acts of renunciation more as a mental attitude. Sarada and her niece Laxmimani were indeed known to have had a north Indian guru, but this was bound to have been more in the nature of a *shiksha guru* than *diksha guru*. Neither of them was formally inducted into a life of *sanyas* and at no stage in their lives did they lead the life of an ascetic. Sarada Devi related to the Ramakrishna movement primarily as a householder and as a devoted wife without overlooking a certain religious standing that naturally followed from this position. This secured for her two tactical advantages. In the first place, it earned for her the support of Ramakrishna's devotees who now saw the Ramakrishna-Sarada movement as a holistic and internally integrated tradition. But this also allowed her to create her own group of followers, if only because she appeared to represent an authentic face of an older tradition. I am prepared to hazard the guess that this also served to create a greater bonding between householder devotees and monks within the Ramakrishna movement. It was because she so faithfully mirrored some of the most vital social and religious ideals of Sri Ramakrishna himself that some monks who had been earlier initiated by Sri Ramakrishna agreed to take a second initiation from his wife. Mahendranath Gupta appears to have served both Ramakrishna and his wife with equal conviction and did not see any potential cause for conflict between the two. After expressing some reservations initially, he gladly accepted Sarada Devi's ruling at the Sevashram in Benares that world-renouncing monks had also to think of active engagement with society. Such fusions helped to promote the idea of a continuously common rhythm and organicity within the movement.

CHRONOLOGY

22 December 1853	Birth at Jairambati as eldest child of Ramchandra Mukhopadhyay and Shyamasundari Devi
May 1859	Marriage and first visit to Kamarpukur
November–December, 1860	Second visit to Kamarpukur
1864	Famine relief work at Jairambati
May 1866	Third visit to Kamarpukur
December 1866–January 1867	Fourth visit to Kamarpukur
May–November 1867	Fifth visit to Kamarpukur; joined by Bhairavi, Hridayram and Ramakrishna
March 1872	First visit to Dakshineswar
5 June 1872	Shodashi Puja at Dakshineswar
March 1874	Death of Ramchandra Mukhopadhyay
April 1874	Second visit to Dakshineswar
1875	Suffers from acute dysentery; Goddess Singha Bahini invoked
November 1875	First Jagaddhatri Puja at Jairambati
February 1876	Death of Chandramani Devi; treatment for enlarged spleen at Kayapat-Badanganj
17 March 1876	Third visit to Dakshineswar
November 1877	Jagaddhatri Puja first organized by Shyamasundari Devi at own residence
February 1878	Fourth visit to Dakshineswar
February 1881	Fifth visit to Dakshineswar; the Telo Bhelo episode*
May–June, 1881	Hriday asked to leave Dakshineswar

February–March, 1882	Sixth visit to Dakshineswar
January 1884	Seventh visit to Dakshineswar
March 1885	Eighth visit to Dakshineswar
April 1885	Ramakrishna falls ill
2 October 1885	Joins Ramakrishna at Shyampukur
11 December 1885	Ramakrshna and Sarada move to Kashipur garden house
16 August 1886	Ramakrishna passes away
August 1886–August 1887	Pilgrimage to Vrindavan and other spots in north India
September 1887	Return to Kamarpukur and hardships
May–June 1887	Resides at Nilambar Mukherjee's garden house at Belur; Swami Abhedananda composes stotra in praise of Sarada Devi
5 November 1888–12 January 1889	Pilgrimage to Puri
February 1889	Visits Antpur
25 March 1890	Visits Gaya and Bodh Gaya
13 April 1890	Death of Balaram Basu
April–May 1891	Girish Chandra Ghosh visits Jairambati
31 May 1893	Vivekananda leaves for USA
June–July 1893	At Nilambar Mukherjee's garden house; performs *panchatapa brata*
February–April 1894	Visits Kailoar
February–May 1895	Second pilgrimage tour of Vrindavan
May 1896	Moves to rented house at Bagbazar
19 February 1897	Vivekananda returns from the West
1 May 1897	Ramakarishna Math and Mission founded
February 1898	Advance paid for acquiring land at Belur
February 1898	Math moved from Alambazar to Nilambar Mukherjee's garden house
17 March 1898	Vivekananda and Western disciples call On Sarada Devi at Bagbazar
April 1898	Construction work at Belur begins

November 1898	Sarada Devi photographed; attends inaugural ceremony for Nivedita's school at Bagbazar
January 1899	Ramakrishna monks start living at Belur
28 March 1899	Death of Swami Yogananda
20 June 1899	Vivekananda begins his second tour of the West
August 1899	Death of brother Abhayacharan
December 1900	Vivekananda returns from the West
October 1901	Vivekananda organizes Durga Puja at Belur; Sarada Devi present
4 July 1902	Vivekananda passes away
February 1904	Sarada Devi moves to a rented place at Bagbazar
November 1904–January 1905	Second pilgrimage tour of Puri
April 1905	Sarada Devi photographed along with Radhu, Laxmimani and others at Chitpore, Calcutta
May 1905	Photographed at Van Dyke Studio at the Behest of Swami Virjananda
January 1906	Death of mother, Shyamasundari Devi
8 July 1906	Death of Gopaler Ma
July 1906	Kedar Das donates land at Bagbazar to Belur Math
October 1907	Sarada Devi attends Durga Puja at the residence of Girish Chandra Ghosh; meets actresses of the Bengali stage
November 1907	Construction work at Bagbazar under way for housing Sarada Devi, Saradananda obtains loan of Rs 5,700
late 1908	Udbodhan Press shifts to new premises at Bagbazar, construction costs Rs 11,000
1909	Sarada Devi travels to Kamarpukur to celebrate birthday festival of Ramakrishna
23 May 1909	Sarada Devi steps into the Udbodhan House
June 1909	Sarada Devi catches small pox

1909	Sister Devmata calls on Sarada Devi
14 December 1910	Additional land next to Udbodhan house acquired at the price of Rs 1,800
February 1911	Visits Balaram Basu's estate at Kothar; reconverts Postmaster Debendranath Chattopadhyay to Hinduism
February–April 1911	Tour of south India
12 May 1911	Last meeting with Nivedita
21 August 1911	Death of Swami Ramakrishnananda
13 October 1911	Nivedita passes away at Darjeeling
October 1911	Attends Durga Puja at Belur for the second time
24 November 1912	Advises swadeshi volunteers at Koalpara Ashram to abide by the teachings of Ramakrishna
16 October 1912	Arrives at Belur on the occasion of Durga Puja; monks pull the horse cart on which she is seated
5 November 1912–16 January 1913	Third tour of Benares
April 1914	Jagadamba Ashram founded at Koalpara
1915	Intense family disputes between brothers over share in family property
May 1916	Special rooms for Sarada Devi built at Jairambati
May 1916	Suffers from high fever at Jairambati
January 1918	Several doctors attend on Sarada Devi; police raid Jairambati and Koalpara in search of political agitators
April–May 1918	Recovery and relapse
30 July 1918 1918	Death of Swami Premananda; the police look for swadeshi volunteers at Koalpara and Jairambati
January 1919–February 1920	Last residence at Jairambati
April 1920	Death of Swami Adbhutananda
May 1920	Dr Prandahan Basu diagnoses her with kala azar

May 1920	Death of brother Baradaprasanna
21 July 1920	Sarada Devi passes away
21 December 1921	Foundation stone laid for Matri Mandir at Belur
1953	Centenary celebrations; special commemorative issue of the journal *Udbodhan* published

*According to Narasingha Sil, the encounter with the dacoit at Telo Bhelo occurred on 17 March 1876. Two reasons cast doubt on this date. First, Sarada Devi recalled that on this particular trip, she was accompanied by Laxmimani Ghatak and Shyamasundari Devi. In all probability, this occurred either in the year 1881 or soon thereafter. Second, the wife of the dacoit reportedly fed Sarada with green peas handpicked from the adjacent fields. Judging by the local weather, this had to be early spring. 17 March appears to be too late to be possible. One cannot also be certain about the number of visits Sarada Devi made to Dakshineswar between 1872 and 1886 or their exact timing. Our two major sources on chronology reveal internal differences.

[**Sources**: Narasingha P. Sil, *Divine Dowager: The Life and Teachings of Saradamani the Holy Mother* (Selingsgrove and London: Susquehanna University Press and Associated University Press, 2003), pp. 15–18; Renuka Chattopadhyay, "Jeebonpanji" in *Yugajanani Sarada*, ed. Swami Purnatmananda (Calcutta: Udbodhan, 2001: 497–511).]

BIBLIOGRAPHY

A Early Obituaries and Short Life Sketches

Reportedly, short obituaries appeared in the August–September 1920 issue of the *Brabuddha Bharata* and the June–July and October–November issues of *Vedanta Kesari*. The short sketch appearing in the September issue of the *Prabuddha Bharata* ("The Holy Mother") was authored by Mahendranath Gupta. Subsequently, two more sketches appeared in the same journal in December 1921 and April 1922. The first of these was titled "Chaitanya", and the latter titled "The Indian Ideal of Womanhood" by Dinesh Maharaj (later Swami Nikhilananda).

In August 1920, Udbodhan published two short obituaries. One of these called "Mayer Kotha" was authored by Saralabala Sarkar and the other was by someone who signed off as "Sree".

A short life sketch of Sarada Devi was authored by Ramananda Chattopadhyay for the Bengali journal *Prabasi* in Baiskah, 1331 BS (April–May 1924). Its English version appeared in *The Modern Review* of June 1927.

Swami Ishanananda claims that Brahmabandhab Upadhyay wrote an article (date not known) in the politically radical paper, *Sandhya*.

The American actress and educationist Winifred Hes (1905–42) wrote a 48-page sketch of Sarada Devi's life titled, *A Holy Mother: Sarada Devi*, posthumously published in 1944.

A short life sketch appeared in the work, *Banglar Dharma Guru*, by Rajendralal Acharya; see Vol. 2 (Calcutta: Student's Library, 1947).

Madhavananda, Swami, and R.C. Mazumdar, ed. *Great Women of India: The Holy Mother Birth Centenary Memorial*. Calcutta: Advaita Ashrama, 1953.

B Full length Biographies

Akshaychaitnya, Brahmachari. *Sri Sri Sarada Devi*. 3rd Edition. Calcutta: Model Publishing House, 1948.

Akshaychaitanya, Brahmachari. *Brahmananda Lilakatha*. 2nd Edition. Calcutta: Nababharat Publications, 1965.

Archanapuri, Sri. *Janani Sarada Devi*. 4th Edition. Calcutta: Satyananada Devayatan, 1992.

Bhumananda, Swami. *Sri Sri Mayer Jeebonkatha*. Calcutta: Sri Ramkrishna Sarada Math, 1986.

Chattopadhyay, Naliniranjan. *Sri Sri Ma Sarada: Kalanukramik Jeeboni O Kathamrita*. Calcutta: Dev Sahitya Kutir, 1959.

Dasgupta, Manadsankar. *Sri Sri Ma Saradamani Devi*. 11th R. Calcutta, 2017.

Devi, Durgapuri. *Sarada Ramakrishna*. Calcutta: Saradeswari Ashram, 1954.

Gambhirananda, Swami. *Sri Ma Sarada Devi: Sri Mayer Shatabarsha Jayanti*. Calcutta: Udbodhan Press, 1954. The English version of the book was published form Mylapore in 1977.

Ghosh, Sukla. *Viswarupini Ma Sarada*. Calcutta: Sri Ramakrishna Vedanta Math, n.d.

Krishnananda, Swami. *Sri Sarada Punthi (Lila Khanda)*. Calcutta: Indian Book Concern, n.d.

Mitra, Ashtosh. *Sri Ma*. Calcutta: The Shyambazar Electric Emporium, 1944.

Muktiprana, Pravrajika. *Sri Ma Sarada*. Dakshineswar: Sri Sarada Math, 1986.

Nikhilananda, Swami. *Holy Mother: Being the life of Sarada Devi, Wife of Sri Ramakrishna and Helpmate in His Mission.* Mylapore: Sri Ramakrishna Math, 1962. The original American edition of the book was published in 1961.

Pavitrananda, Swami. *A Short Life of the Holy Mother.* Calcutta: Advaita Ashrama, 1942.

Prabhananda, Swami. *Sri Sri Sarada Mahima.* Calcutta: Udbodhan Press, 2019.

Purnatmananda, Swami. *Chirantani Sarada.* Calcutta: Udbodhan Press, 1997.

Sengupta, Achintyakumar. *Paramaprakriti Sri Sri Saradamani.* Calcutta: Signet Press, 1954.

Sengupta, Purba. *Janani Sarada Devi: Udbhashita Jyoti.* Calcutta: Udbodhan Press, 1953.

Sil, Narasingha P. "Saradamani's Holy Motherhood. A Reappraisal." In *Asian Journal of Woman's Studies* 4.1(1996): 53–76.

Sil, Narasingha P. *Divine Dowager: The Life and Teachings of Saradamani the Holy Mother.* Selingsgrove and London: Susquehanna University Press and Associated Press, 2003.

Teachings of Sri Sarada Devi: The Holy Mother (Being the Life and Teachings of One Whose Mission it was to Reveal the Motherhood of God). Mylapore: Ramakrishna Math, 1949.

Tapasyananda, Swami. *Sri Sarada Devi. The Holy Mother.* Mylapore: Ramakrishna Math, 1940.

C Memoirs and Reminiscences

Abhedananda, Swami. *Amar Jeebon Katha.* Calcutta: Ramakrishna Vedanta Math, 1957.

Arupananda, Swami, ed. *Sri Sri Mayer Katha.* 2 Parts. Calcutta. Udbodhan Press, 1926 and 1937 respectively.

Chetananda, Swami. *Matridarshan.* Calcutta: Udbodhan Press, 1997.

Dasgupta, Abhaya. "Sarada, the Mother of the World." In *Prabuddha Bharata* 95.4 (April 1990).

Hiranmayananda, Swami, ed. *Sri Sarada Devi, The Great Wonder: A Compilation of Revelations, Reminiscences and Studies.* New Delhi: Ramakrishna Mission, 1984.

Ishanananda, Swami. *Matri Sannidhye.* Calcutta: Udbodhan Press, 2001.

Lokeswarananda, Swami, ed. *Shatarupe Sarada.* Calcutta: Ramakrishna Mission Institute of Culture, 1984.

Purnatmananda, Swami, ed. *Sri Sri Mayer Padaprante.* 4 volumes. Calcutta: Udbodhan Press, 1994–2003. The English translation of the work is available as *Reminscences of Sri Sarada Devi by monks, devotees and others.* Translated by Maloti Sen Gupta. Calcutta: Advaita Ashram, 2014.

Purnanatmananda, Swami, ed. *Yugajanai Sarada.* Calcutta: Udbodhan Press, 1997.

Roy, Motilal. *Sri Sri Thakur Ramkrishner Dampataya Jeebon.* Calcutta: Pravartak Publishing House, 1930.

Sen, Kumud Bandhu. *Reminiscences of the Holy Mother.* Serialized in *Prabuddha Bharata*, May 1953 and August–September 1956.

Sister Nivedita. *The Master as I saw Him.* Calcutta: Udbodhan Press, 1910.

Sivaprabhananda, Swami, ed. *Sri Ma Sarada O Tapobhumi Kothar.* Calcutta: Udbodhan Press, 2016.

Sri Ma Sarada Devi: Alokchitre Jeebonkatha. Calcutta: Udbodhan Press, 1990.

Sri Sri Ma Shatavarsha Jayanti Samkhya. Calcutta: Udbodhan Press, 1954. The English translation of this work was published as *Gospel of the Holy Mother: Recorded by Her Devotee Children*, Madras: 1984.

Vednatprana, Pravrajika and Sadatmaprana, Pravrajika, eds. *Jonmojanmantarer Ma*. Dakshineswar: Sri Sarada Math, 1997.

D Articles

Bevilaqua, Daniela. "Are Women entitled to become ascetics?" in International Journal of Afro Asiatic Studies 21 (2017): 51–79.

Ganesh, Kamala. "Mother who is not a mother. In Search of the Great Indian Goddess." In *Economic and Political Weekly* 25, no. 42–43 (October 1990): 58–64.

Ganeshananda, Swami. "How the Holy Mother Influences her Western Devotees." In *Prabuddha Bharata* 89 (Decmeber 1984): 491–97.

"Holy Mother-Ideal of Womanhood" in *Prabuddha Bharata* 44 (December 1989): 482–91.

Khandelwal, Meena. "Ungendered Atma, Masculine Virility and Feminine Compassion: Ambiguities in Renunciant Discourse on Gender." In *Contributions to Indian Sociology* 21, no.1 (1997): 79–107.

Mandavia, Chetna: "Sri Sarada Devi. An Ideal for Indian Women." In *Prabuddha Bharata* 45 (December 1990): 500–6.

McLean, Malcolm D. "Women as Aspects of the Mother Goddess: A Case Study of Ramakrishna." In *Religion* 19 (1989): 13–26.

Mozumdar, P.C. "The Emacipation of Women in Bengal." In *The Calcutta Review* (April 1904): 125–31.

Mumukshananda, Swami. "Srisrima: Prachin Adarsher shesh Pratinidhi ebam Nabin Adarsher Agradut." In Swami Lokeshwarananda ed. *Shatarupe Sarada*. Calcutta: RMIC, 1989, pp. 587–608.

Ojha, Catherine Clementine. "Feminine Asceticism in Hinduism: Its Tradition and Present Condition." In *Man in India* 61, no.3 (September 1981): 254–85.

Ojha, Catherine Clementine. "Outside the Norm. Women Ascetics in Hindu Society." In *Economic and Political Weekly* 23, no.18 (30 April 1988): 34–36.

Prabuddhaprana, Pravrajika. "Holy Mother: The Ideal of Indian Motherhood as depicted in the Prabuddha Bharata." In *Prabuddha Bharata* 76 (January 2021): 124–30.

Roy, Shreela. "Life and Teachings of Holy Mother Sri Sarada Devi: The Relevance for the Modern Indian Woman." In *Bulletin of the Ramakrishna Mission Institute of Culture* 35, no.12 (December 1984): 272–77.

Rustau, Hiltrud. "The Ramakrishna Mission. Its Female Aspect." In Antony Copley ed. *Gurus and Their Followers: New Religious Movements in Colonial India*. Delhi: Oxford University Press, 2000.

E General Works

Asheshaprana, Pravrajika. *Ananya Sudhira*. Dakshineswar. 2nd Reprint. Ramakrishna Sarada Mission, 2019.

Atmananda, Swami, trans. *The Essential Sri Anandamayi Ma: Life and Teachings of a 20th-Century Saint, Biography by Alexander Lipski & Words of Sri Anandamayi Ma*. Edited by Joseph A. Fitzgerald. Delhi: Motilal Banarasidass Publishers, 2010 (Indian Edition).

Nirbhayaprana, Pravarajika, ed. *Bharatiprana Smritikatha*. 2nd Edition. Dakshineswar: Sri Sarada Math, 2013.

Prabuddhaprana, Pravrajika. *Saint Sara: The Life of Sara Chapman Bull*. 2nd Edition. Dakshineswar: Sri Sarada Math, 2014.

Prabuddhaprana, Pravrajika. *Tantine: The Life of Josephine McLeod. Friend of Swami Vivekananda.* 3rd Edition. Dakshineswar: Sri Sarada Math, 2008.

Rukmani, T.S. *Sanyasis in the Hindu Tradition: Changing Perspectives.* Delhi: D.K. Print World, Pvt. Ltd, 2011.

Sen, Amiya P. *Three Essays on Sri Ramakrishna and His Times.* Shimla: Indian Institute of Advanced Study, 2001.

Sen, Amiya P. *Ramakrishna Paramahamsa: The Sadhaka of Dakshineswar.* Delhi: Penguin Viking, 2010.

Stavig, Gopal. *Western Admirers of Ramakrishna and His Disciples.* Ed. Swami Shuddhidananda. Calcutta: Advaita Ashrama, 2010.

F Unpublished Dissertations

Goulet, Trishia Nicole. "The Lives of Sarada Devi: Gender Renunciation and Hindu Politics in Colonial India." Unpublished PhD Dissertation, Department of Religion, University of Manitoba, Winnipeg, 2009.

Robinson, Betty Sue. "The Ramakrishna Sarada Math: A Study of a Women's Movement in Bengal." PhD Dissertation, Columbia University, 1978.

OTHER PUBLISHED BOOKS

in this new series

Charu Majumdar: *The Dreamer Rebel*

Heisnam Sabitri: *The Way of the Thamoi*

Homi J Bhabha: *A Renaissance Man among Scientists*

Jamini Roy: *A Painter Who Revisited the Roots*

RK Laxman: *Back with a Punch*

Muthulakshmi Reddy: *A Trailblazer in Surgery and Women's Rights*

Rani Gaidinliu: *Legendary Freedom Fighter from the North East*